LIFE
APPLICATION®
BIBLE
COMMENTARY

EPHESIANS

Bruce B. Barton, D.Min.
Philip Comfort, Ph.D.
Kent Keller, M.Div.
Linda K. Taylor
Dave Veerman, M.Div.

Series Editor: Grant Osborne, Ph.D.
Editor: Philip Comfort, Ph.D.

Tyndale House Publishers, Inc.
CAROL STREAM, ILLINOIS

Visit Tyndale's exciting Web site at www.tyndale.com

Ephesians

Copyright © 1996 by The Livingstone Corporation. All rights reserved.

Contributing Editors: James C. Galvin, Ed.D., and Ronald A. Beers

Library of Congress Cataloging-in-Publication Data

Ephesians / Bruce B. Barton . . . [et al.] ; editor, Philip Comfort.
    p.   cm. — (Life Application Bible commentary)
Includes bibliographical references and index.
ISBN-13: 978-0-8423-2813-5 (soft cover : alk. paper)
ISBN-10: 0-8423-2813-0 (soft cover : alk. paper)
  1. Bible. N.T. Ephesians—Commentaries. I. Barton, Bruce B.
II. Comfort, Philip Wesley. III. Series.
BS2695.3.E63 1996
227′.507—dc20   96-31517

Printed in the United States of America

10 09 08 07
16 15 14 13 12 11 10

CONTENTS

Gospels

MATTHEW
MARK: between
LUKE

ACTS

Paul's Epistles

ROMANS: about 57
1 CORINTHIANS: about 55
2 CORINTHIANS: about 56–57
GALATIANS: about 49

EPHESIANS
PHILIPPIANS
COLOSSIANS
1 THESSALONIANS: about 51
2 THESSALONIANS: about 51–52
1 TIMOTHY
2 TIMOTHY
TITUS
PHILEMON

General Epistles JAMES: about 49

1 PETER
2 PETER

JUDE

NEW TESTAMENT

| AD 30 | 40 | 50 | 60 |

The church
begins
(Acts 1)

35
Paul's
conversion
(Acts 9)

46
Paul's first
missionary
journey
(Acts 13)

Jerusalem Council
and Paul's second
journey (Acts 15)

54
Paul's
third
journey
(Acts 18)
Nero
becomes
emperor

58
Paul
arrested
(Acts 21)

64
Rome
burns

61–63
Paul's
Roman
imprison
ment
(Acts 28

etween 60–65
5–65
bout 60

bout 63–65

JOHN: probably 80–85

bout 61
bout 62
bout 61

bout 64
bout 66–67
bout 64
bout 61

HEBREWS: probably before 70

bout 62–64
bout 67

1 JOHN: between 85–90
2 JOHN: about 90
3 JOHN: about 90

bout 65

REVELATION: about 95

TIMELINE

| 70 | 80 | 90 | 100 |

7–68
*Paul and
Peter
executed*

Jerusalem
destroyed

79 *Mt. Vesuvius
erupts in Italy*

68
*Essenes hide
their library
of Bible
manuscripts
in a cave
in Qumran
by the
Dead Sea*

About 75
*John begins
ministry in
Ephesus*

75
*Rome begins
construction
of Colosseum*

About 98
*John's
death
at Ephesus*

FOREWORD

The *Life Application Bible* Commentary series provides verse-by-verse explanation, background, and application for every verse in the New Testament. In addition, it gives personal help, teaching notes, and sermon ideas that will address needs, answer questions, and provide insight for applying God's Word to life today. The content is highlighted so that particular verses and phrases are easy to find.

Each volume contains three sections: introduction, commentary, and reference. The introduction includes an overview of the book, the book's historical context, a timeline, cultural background information, major themes, an overview map, and an explanation about the author and audience.

The commentary section includes running commentary on the Bible text with reference to several modern versions, especially the New International Version and the New Revised Standard Version, accompanied by life applications interspersed throughout. Additional elements include charts, diagrams, maps, and illustrations. There are also insightful quotes from church leaders and theologians such as John Calvin, Martin Luther, John Wesley, and A. W. Tozer. These features are designed to help you quickly grasp the biblical information and be prepared to communicate it to others. The reference section includes an index and a bibliography.

INTRODUCTION

What builds a friendship? Certainly common values, ideals, and experiences help. But friendship also needs mutual appreciation and respect, vulnerability, and spending many hours together. And shared experiences bond people—especially experiences of suffering together and working together to reach a common goal.

Of all the churches planted and visited along Paul's missionary journeys, he enjoyed a very close relationship with the church at Ephesus. Paul first visited the city briefly on his way home to Jerusalem (A.D. 53), but he promised to return (Acts 18:19-21). He did, just one year later, on his third missionary journey. This time, Paul lived and ministered in the city for three years (Acts 20:31). During these stays in Ephesus, Paul developed close relationships with the believers there. Paul taught about the Holy Spirit (Acts 19:1-7), encountered opposition in the synagogue (Acts 19:8-9), and held an open forum in a lecture hall for seekers from all over the province of Asia (Acts 19:9-10). He healed the sick and cast out demons (Acts 19:11-12). Many confessed their sins and turned to Christ (Acts 19:13-20). Paul became a controversial figure, incurring the anger of many Greek businessmen and Jews. In fact, the silversmith Demetrius stirred up a riot against Paul and his traveling companions (Acts 19:23-41). Paul's enemies were as ferocious as wild beasts (1 Corinthians 15:32). No wonder Paul and the Ephesian believers were close.

To underscore this close relationship, consider the farewell scene between Paul and the elders of the Ephesian church as Paul was about to leave for Jerusalem. Listen to his final instructions to them at Miletus, recorded in Acts 20:18-35.

When they arrived, he said to them: "You know how I lived the whole time I was with you, from the first day I came into the province of Asia. I served the Lord with great humility and with tears, although I was severely tested by the plots of the Jews. You know that I have not hesitated to preach anything that would be helpful to you but have taught you publicly and from house to house. I have declared to both Jews and Greeks that they must turn to God in repentance and have faith in our Lord Jesus.

"And now, compelled by the Spirit, I am going to Jerusalem, not knowing what will happen to me there. I only know that in every city the Holy Spirit warns me that prison and hardships are facing me. However, I consider my life worth nothing to me, if only I may finish the race and complete the task the Lord Jesus has given me—the task of testifying to the gospel of God's grace.

"Now I know that none of you among whom I have gone about preaching the kingdom will ever see me again. Therefore, I declare to you today that I am innocent of the blood of all men. For I have not hesitated to proclaim to you the whole will of God. Keep watch over yourselves and all the flock of which the Holy Spirit has made you overseers. Be shepherds of the church of God, which he bought with his own blood. I know that after I leave, savage wolves will come in among you and will not spare the flock. Even from your own number men will arise and distort the truth in order to draw away disciples after them. So be on your guard! Remember that for three years I never stopped warning each of you night and day with tears.

"Now I commit you to God and to the word of his grace, which can build you up and give you an inheritance among all those who are sanctified. I have not coveted anyone's silver or gold or clothing. You yourselves know that these hands of mine have supplied my own needs and the needs of my companions. In everything I did, I showed you that by this kind of hard work we must help the weak, remembering the words the Lord Jesus himself said: 'It is more blessed to give than to receive.'"
(Acts 20:18-35 NIV)

As you read Ephesians, see this book as more than an important, theological document for an ancient church. It is the Holy Spirit-inspired letter to followers of Christ with whom Paul had lived and worked for three years. He was committed to them and to the churches in that area. This is a letter bathed in love.

How committed are you to those whom you have taught and led? What can you do to encourage them in their walk with Christ?

AUTHOR

Paul: apostle of Christ, courageous missionary, gifted teacher, articulate apologist, and Christian statesman.

Two major headings in this book (1:1 and 3:1) show that this epistle claims to have been written by Paul the apostle. This claim is confirmed by many church fathers, including Polycarp, Origen, Irenaeus, Clement of Alexandria, and Tertullian. Most scholars throughout the history of the church have affirmed the same. But some modern scholars have questioned Paul's authorship of Ephesians primarily because Ephesians bears so much resemblance to Colossians, which they consider to have been written by Paul prior to the composition of Ephesians. These critics reason that Paul would have not repeated himself so frequently and even changed definitions for certain key terms, such as "mystery," "economy," and "fullness." Thus, they consider Ephesians to be the work of an imitator, who was definitely an admirer of Paul and one well versed in Pauline style. Furthermore, the critics say that Ephesians has wording that makes it sound as if Paul did not know his readers. For example, in 1:15, Paul wrote, "Ever since I heard about your faith" (NIV); in 3:2, "Surely you have heard about . . ." (NIV); and in 4:21, "Surely you heard of [Christ] and were taught in him in accordance with the truth that is in Jesus" (NIV).

However, many scholars have countered the arguments of the critics of Pauline authorship by pointing out that the similarity of style and wording between Colossians and Ephesians shows a common author, who could be none other than Paul. Indeed, Paul wrote the two epistles within a year's time (A.D. 60–61), making it very natural for him to use similar terminology in both—with particular variation for contextual and audience concerns. Some of the more noteworthy similarities are noted below:

Ephesians	Colossians
1:7	1:14
1:10	1:20
1:19; 2:5	2:12-13
3:2	1:25
4:2-4	3:12-15
4:16	2:19
4:22-24	3:9-10
4:32	3:13
5:6-8	3:6-8
5:15-16	4:5
5:19	3:16
5:20-33	3:17-18
6:19-20	4:3-4
6:22	4:8

Furthermore, scholars counter the argument that the writer of Ephesians didn't seem to know his readers by demonstrating that Ephesians was an encyclical epistle, intended to be read by an audience much greater than Ephesus, though it included Ephesus (see the discussion under "Audience" below).

AUDIENCE

The churches in Ephesus and the surrounding area.

The city. Outside of Rome, Ephesus was the most important city that Paul visited. Located at the intersection of two ancient, major overland routes (the coastal road running north to Troas and the western route to Colosse, Laodicea, and beyond) at the western edge of Asia Minor (now Turkey), with easy access to the Aegean Sea, Ephesus had become a political, commercial, and religious center. It had been one of the main routes either by sea or by land from Rome to the East. Ephesus had a harbor on the Cayster River which emptied into the Aegean Sea, so the city, at one time, was known as "the Landing Place," and the citizens were proud of its role as a port city and a gateway to Asia. By the first century, however, the harbor was nearly filled with silt, thus causing some economic decline.

A strong source of income for Ephesus was the great temple of Artemis (Diana), the fertility goddess. Four times larger than the Parthenon, this shrine, considered one of the seven wonders of the ancient world, was reverenced throughout "all Asia and the world" (Acts 19:27 NRSV). The temple stood outside the city walls and faced east. Built completely of marble, it was 324 feet long and 164 feet wide and took 220 years to erect. The image of the goddess stood, surrounded by curtains, in the center of the temple.

In addition to the temple, Ephesus had an immense amphitheater (see Acts 19:27-29) that could seat more than twenty-five thousand spectators. The city was positioned between two mountainous ridges. The eastern ridge formed the foundation for this theater, as it had been cut out of the mountainside. Nearby stood the stadium, or race course, where fights between wild animals or between men and animals were held. A great marble street, the main street of Ephesus, ran northwest from the theater to the harbor. The street was flanked on both sides by an elaborate colonnade.

The city's commercial life and prosperity came to depend on the many thousands of tourists and worshipers visiting the temple, theater, and stadium annually. No wonder the populace became alarmed, and then enraged, when told that Paul's teachings would undermine the worship of Artemis and thus endanger their livelihood and the city's economy (Acts 19:23-41).

The church. As was his custom, Paul began his ministry in Ephesus among Jews, in the synagogue (Acts 19:8). When the Jewish leaders refused to listen, Paul left and taught in a rented lecture hall (Acts 19:9-10). During the next two years, many Jews and Greeks came to hear the gospel and believed (Acts 19:11, 17). At the writing of this letter, the church consisted mostly of Gentiles (2:11-19; 3:1).

The church at Ephesus flourished and became a strong spiritual community. Apollos had taught there and had been instructed by Priscilla and Aquila (Acts 18:24-28). Paul left the Ephesian church under the care of competent elders (Acts 20:17), and later, he commissioned Timothy to minister there (1 Timothy 1:3). Scholars believe that the apostle John wrote his letters and his Gospel from Ephesus (A.D. 85–90). After John's exile on Patmos, he returned to Ephesus for his final years (A.D. 100). Irenaeus (A.D. 120–202) wrote, "Afterwards, John, the disciple of the Lord, who also had leaned upon his breast, did himself publish a gospel during his residence at Ephesus in Asia."

In addition to having hosted these great spiritual leaders, the church in Ephesus is mentioned in the book of Revelation. God commends the believers for their "deeds," "hard work," and "perseverance" (Revelation 2:2-3 NIV), but he warns them about forsaking their "first love" and calls them to "repent and do the things you did at first" (Revelation 2:4-5 NIV).

Certainly this was a remarkable church.

The recipients. Most likely, this letter was addressed to several churches in the district around Ephesus—namely, the Roman province of Asia (commonly known as Asia Minor). Called the Epistle to the Ephesians, the letter was not really intended to be only for the church at Ephesus. Most modern scholars are convinced that it was an encyclical (circular letter), meant for many churches in Asia, including Ephesus. There are several reasons to affirm this. First, the earliest manuscripts (the Chester Beatty Papyrus—P46, Codex Sinaiticus, and Codex Vaticanus) do not contain the words "in Ephesus" in Ephesians 1:1. It appears that Paul purposely left the name of the locality out so it could be filled in later as the letter circulated to each locality. (The Greek construction in 1:1 calls for a prepositional phrase designating a locality to be present in the sentence.) Since Ephesus was the leading city of Asia, it would be quite natural for scribes to assign this letter to the church at Ephesus. Second, the Epistle to the Ephesians has all the marks of being a general treatise rather than a personal letter to a specific local church. Paul had lived with the believers at Ephesus for three years (Acts 20:31). He knew them intimately, yet in this epistle, there are no personal greetings or specific exhortations. When we consider Paul's manner in many of his other letters, it would be quite unlike him to have excluded these personal expressions. Quite the contrary, Paul speaks to the saints whom he has only *heard* about and who have only *heard* about him (see 1:15; 3:2).

It is possible that this epistle was the one mentioned by Paul in Colossians 4:15-16, wherein Paul encourages the church in Colosse to exchange letters with the church in Laodicea—exhorting the church in Colosse to "read the letter from Laodicea." This doesn't mean that this epistle was written by the Laodiceans or that it was written from Laodicea, just that it was circulating among the churches in Asia Minor and would naturally come to Colosse after Laodicea. The two cities are just a few miles apart. Thus, it is not difficult to reconstruct the route that this circular letter took. By using Revelation 2–3 as a model, it seems likely that the epistle traveled first to Ephesus, then to Smyrna, Pergamum, Thyatira, Sardis, Philadelphia, Laodicea, and finally, Colosse. Of course, it could have gone to other churches en route, but this is a likely re-creation. Tychicus brought the letter from Rome to Ephesus (see 6:21). From there it would have circulated counterclockwise throughout the churches in Asia Minor—in the same manner that the book of Revelation traveled. As the first and leading city in the area, it would have been natural for the name Ephesus to be attached to this epistle. However, the design of such an encyclical was that the name of each locality was to be filled in as the letter circulated. In modern times, this would be like personalizing an office memo sent by E-mail to several people. As was mentioned earlier, the three earliest manuscripts preserve the document in its pristine form for this opening verse—by leaving out the name of the locality. Other later manuscripts preserve it in one of its later forms, where "in Ephesus" has been filled in.

Paul's first visit to Ephesus (on the seacoast of Lydia, near the river Cayster) is described in Acts 18:19-21. The work, begun by his disputations with the Jews in his short visit, was carried on by Apollos, Aquila, and Priscilla (Acts 18:24-26). During Paul's second visit, he remained at Ephesus "three years" (Acts 19:10—the "two years" in this verse are only *part* of the time—and Acts 20:31). Paul used Ephesus as a center for proclaiming the gospel throughout the entire region. He did this by renting a lecture hall from Tyrannus where he would spend every afternoon teaching the Scriptures. As a result, people from all around Asia Minor came to Ephesus to hear Paul (Acts 19:9-10), and consequently many became believers. One such person was Philemon, an elder at Colosse. Since there is no record of Paul's having gone to Colosse, it is likely that Philemon (and others) heard the Word from Paul in Ephesus, became believers, and then returned home to Colosse to begin the church life there.

This situation helps us understand why Paul's message in this letter is both intimate and global. Intimate—because of his close association with the Ephesians. Global—because the truths he wanted to communicate were for all the churches. And this is why Ephesians has had such an appeal to all believers throughout the church age. Next to Paul's Epistle to the Romans, this is the one epistle that could also be called a treatise rather than an occasional letter. Ephesians presents the grand picture of God's eternal purpose for the Christian church.

SETTING AND DATE

Written about A.D. 61, from Rome, during Paul's imprisonment there.

Paul had been a Christian for nearly thirty years by the time he wrote this letter. He had taken three missionary trips and had established churches all around the Mediterranean Sea. At the end of his third journey, he was arrested in Jerusalem for causing a riot with his preaching. Paul was committed to going to Rome (Acts 19:21), and God told him that he would go there and preach the gospel (Acts 23:11). So, upon his arrest, Paul appealed to Caesar and eventually did arrive in Rome, the capital of the Empire (read the story in Acts 21:27–28:31). Paul probably hadn't planned on being in prison during his ministry there, but that didn't stop him from preaching and teaching.

In Rome, Paul was under house arrest, meaning that he was not really in a prison but probably under guard in a minimum security situation while awaiting trial. There was no threat of his trying to escape; Paul was right where he wanted to be. People from all over the Empire made their way to Rome. Though a prisoner, Paul was free to have visitors and to write letters (see Acts 28:16ff.). Those who heard the gospel could take it, for

Paul, to the ends of the earth (Acts 1:8). "For two whole years Paul stayed [in Rome] in his own rented house and welcomed all who came to see him. Boldly and without hindrance he preached the kingdom of God and taught about the Lord Jesus Christ" (Acts 28:30 NIV).

While under house arrest, Paul preached to Jews and Gentiles alike, witnessing to the whole Roman guard (Philippians 1:13) and helping Roman believers grow in their faith. He also wrote four letters that are commonly called his Prison Epistles: Ephesians, Colossians, Philippians, and Philemon. Timothy often visited Paul (Philippians 1:1; Colossians 1:1; Philemon 1), as did Tychicus (Ephesians 6:21), Epaphroditus (Philippians 4:18), and Mark (Colossians 4:10).

This epistle was addressed to the Ephesians and other Christians in the area (see discussion above under "Audience") and was written during the early part of this imprisonment at Rome. It was probably written immediately after his epistle to the Colossians, which bears a close resemblance in many passages, the apostle having in his mind generally the same great truths in writing both. It is an undesigned proof of genuineness that the two epistles, written about the same date and under the same circumstances, display a closer mutual resemblance than those written at distant dates and on different occasions.

Tychicus and Onesimus were sent by Paul to Colosse. Tychicus carried the two epistles to the two churches respectively (Ephesians 6:22; Colossians 4:7)—Ephesians as an encyclical and Colossians as a specific letter. Onesimus carried a letter of recommendation from Paul to Philemon, his former master, residing at Colosse. The date was probably about four years after Paul's parting with the Ephesian elders at Miletus (Acts 20), about A.D. 61. From 6:19-20 it is plain that although he was a prisoner, Paul had some degree of freedom in preaching. This agrees with Acts 28:23, 30-31. Paul's house arrest began in A.D. 60 or 61 and lasted two whole years (Acts 28:30) at least, and perhaps longer.

OCCASION AND PURPOSE

To strengthen the believers in their Christian faith by explaining the nature and purpose of the church, the body of Christ.

Paul felt keenly responsible for the spiritual health of the churches that he had planted. His deep concern led him to revisit many of those churches on subsequent travels, and it certainly motivated him to write letters and to send other teachers and leaders after him. In Paul's parting words to the Ephesian elders, he urged them: "Be shepherds of the church of God, which he bought with his own blood. I know that after I leave, savage wolves will come in among you and will not spare the flock. Even from your own number men will arise and distort the truth in order to draw away disciples after them. So be on your guard!" (Acts 20:28b-31a NIV).

Paul knew that young believers, like little lambs, would be easy prey for false teachers and egotistical preachers—the "savage wolves" who could devastate the flock. So Paul wrote to strengthen and mature his Christian brothers and sisters in their faith by explaining the purpose and power of the church—helping them see the big picture—and by calling believers to sound doctrine and holy living.

The Epistle to the Ephesians can be considered Paul's treatise on the universal church, the body of Christ. Thus, unencumbered with local problems, his description soars high above any mundane affairs and takes us into heaven, where we are presented with a heavenly view of the church as it fits into God's eternal plan.

In this epistle Paul paints the church with multifarious splendor. He depicts her as God's inheritance (1:11); Christ's body, his fullness (1:22-23); God's masterpiece (2:10); the one new person (2:15); the household of God (2:19); the habitation of God (2:21-22); the joint body comprised of Jewish and Gentile believers (3:6); the vessel for God to display his wisdom (3:10); the body equaling Christ's full stature (4:12-13); the full-grown, perfect person (4:13); the bride of Christ (5:23-32); the object of Christ's love (5:25); the very members of Christ's body (5:30); and God's warrior against Satan (6:11-18).

This kaleidoscopic presentation shows that the church is one entity with numerous functions. It serves the Trinity, provides the avenue for unity among people, and opposes God's enemy Satan.

Paul wanted his readers to see God's eternal purpose for the church. With such a high calling and privilege, believers, as individuals and as a local group, should settle for nothing less. In addition, Paul claimed to have received a revelation about the church that had never before been known—that the church would be comprised of both Jewish and Gentile believers, sharing equal status in the body as coheirs, comembers of the body, and joint partakers. He wrote about this revelation so that all the believers could understand his knowledge in "the mystery of Christ," which is the church (see 3:1-9).

Today, many Christians take their faith and their church for granted. Thus, they become critical of fellow believers, the worship services, and church leaders, and often they become susceptible to wrong doctrines. As you read Ephesians, examine your attitudes in light of Paul's description of the church, the body of Christ. And consider how you might encourage and strengthen fellow believers and spiritual leaders.

MESSAGE

God's purpose, Christ the center, The living church, The new family, Christian conduct.

God's purpose (1:3-14, 18-23; 2:6-10). According to God's eternal and loving plan, he directs, carries out, and sustains our salvation. God chose believers "before the creation of the world" and "predestined us to be adopted as his sons" (1:4-5 NIV). Everything happens according to God's eternal purpose (1:11).

Using his Son as the model and prototype, God decided to make more sons just like his beloved Son. This decision emanated from a deep desire in the heart of God to have many children who would be like his beloved Son. Paul used a Greek word in 1:5, 9, and 11 that conveys the idea of desire, even heart's desire. The word is usually translated as "will"—"the will of God." But the English word "will" sublimates the primary meaning. The Greek word *(thelema)* is primarily an emotional word and secondarily volitional. "God's will" is not so much "God's intention" as it is "God's heart's desire." God does have an intention, a purpose, a plan. It is called *prothesis* in Greek (see 1:11), and it literally means "a laying out beforehand" (like a blueprint). This plan was created by God's counsel (called *boule* in Greek, 1:11). Behind the plan and the counsel, however, was not just a mastermind but a heart, a heart of love and of good pleasure. Therefore, Paul talks about "the good pleasure of God's heart's desire" (1:5). Paul also says that God made known to us the mystery of his heart's desire, according to his good pleasure, which he purposed in him (1:9). Indeed, God operates all things according to the counsel of his heart's desire (1:11).

The impetus of God's eternal purpose came from a heart's desire, and that heart's desire was to have many children ("sons") made like his only Son (see Romans 8:28-29). In love, he predestined many people to participate in this "sonship"—not by their own merits but by virtue of being in the Son (1:4-5).

Importance for today. Knowing that we have been chosen

before Creation to receive God's salvation and eternal life and
to be his very own children should energize our gratitude and
boost our self-esteem. Think of it—we have been chosen by
God! Knowing of God's plan and work should not fill us with
pride, however, for his choice of us was totally by grace. We
had no credentials, characteristics, or good works that could
earn his favor. Instead, the proper response is thanksgiving and
humility.

The reality of God's perfect plan should also motivate us to
trust him in every area of life, with his purpose becoming our
mission. How have you responded to God's sovereign plan?
Have you committed yourself to fulfilling God's purpose?

Christ the center (1:19-23; 2:19-22; 3:10-11, 20-21; 4:7-16).
Christ is exalted as the central meaning of the universe and the
focus of history (1:20-23). He is the head of the body, the church
(2:19-22; 4:15-16). He is the Creator and Sustainer of all creation
(1:22-23).

Ephesians presents the church as God's masterpiece (2:10),
his most splendid work of art. God did not create with clay or
canvas and paint. No, everything was created in Christ. God's
Son is the substance of this masterpiece. And everything in
God's new creation was created *for Christ*—he is the recipient
of God's masterpiece.

Notice how often in Ephesians 1 Paul wrote of the believers'
position "in him." Outside of him (the Son), no one could be a
child of God, and no one could be pleasing to the Father. The
many children owe all their divine privileges to the Beloved,
as ones graced in him (1:6). If it were not for God's satisfaction
in his beloved Son, there would not have been the inspiration
for the creation of Adam in the first place. Human beings exist
because God wanted to obtain many more children, each bearing the image of God's unique Son. Men and women please
God and bring him satisfaction by being united to the One who
has always satisfied him. Apart from the Son, we have no
access, no right to sonship. Christ is our unique way to the
Father.

Importance for today. Because Christ is central to everything, he must be central in us—our highest value and the
focus of our lives. In our high-tech, materialistic, relationship-
driven, and sex-oriented society, many idols and values com-
pete for our devotion. It becomes easy to be enticed and drawn
away or to have our lives cluttered by trivial pursuits. But
Christ must be at the center, receiving our total devotion and
ordering our priorities. Keep your focus on him and place all

your interests, relationships, desires, possessions, and goals under his control.

What competes with Christ for your attention? What can you do to keep him at the center of your life?

The living church (1:2-23; 2:1-22; 4:4-6, 11-16). Ephesians includes a masterful and profound description of the church. The church, under Christ's control, is a living body, a family, a dwelling. And God gives believers, by his Holy Spirit, spiritual gifts—special abilities to build the church.

The church is Christ's body to carry out the work he began on earth. He is the head of his body, directing it and motivating it to complete his ministry on earth (1:22-23). As such, the church is the continuation of Christ's incarnation—in the sense that Christ, through another human body, still lives and works on earth among human beings in a tangible, palpable way. But it takes all the members of the body working together in harmony to fulfill the designs and desires of the head (4:4-6, 15-16). This is why there are so many appeals in this epistle for unity and collective maturity. The body must match the head so that Christ can be fully expressed!

The church can cure all the divisiveness among people on earth. Outside of the church, there is no other organization that can offer true equanimity, solidarity, and unity. God designed the church to be the great leveler because all the members are crucified in Christ and start afresh in the risen Christ with equal status as children of God (2:11-16). In the church, there are no hierarchies of sex, race, or occupation. Males are not better than females, Jews better than Gentiles, or freemen better than slaves. All alike died with Christ and were created afresh as "one new person" (2:15 NLT). In the church no one is a stranger, an alien, or a foreigner (2:12-14). All have equal status as joint heirs of the promises of God in Christ Jesus. All are equal members of the body, experiencing the greatest solidarity known to humankind. And all are coparticipants in the benefits of being members of Christ's church (3:6). Only that which was created by God could provide for such unity among human beings. All human efforts to unify people have ultimately and miserably failed.

The church is also Christ's bride. This aspect of the church shows that the Father cares for the deepest needs of his Son. Just as God noticed that Adam was incomplete without a wife (Genesis 2:18), so God realized that Christ needed a loving bride. Thus, God created the church to be both the body and bride of his Son in the same way that Eve was taken from Adam's body. As such, the oneness between husband and wife is extremely intimate (5:25-32). With his bride, Christ enjoys both giving and receiving love.

Importance for today. Paul's presentation of the church reached its pinnacle in this epistle. The church he pictured with words was the church in ideal perfection, the church as seen from heaven—but not yet manifested on earth in fullness. There have been real expressions of this church throughout history, but most would agree that the church has not yet reached "the measure of all the fullness of God" (3:19 NIV)—nor is it yet the glorious church without spot or blemish. But there is the expectation that the church will grow and grow until its manifestation matches the image (4:14-16).

Today we must ask God—as Paul did—that he open the eyes of our heart to catch a vision of what God wants for his church (1:17-18). Then we need to ask that he strengthen us in our spirits so that we, together, can experience all the riches of Christ and thereby display God's fullness in the church. And we also need to exercise all the God-given ministries for the purpose of equipping the believers to do the work of building up the church—until the day we "all reach unity in the faith and in the knowledge of the Son of God and become mature, attaining to the whole measure of the fullness of Christ" (4:13 NIV).

As part of Christ's body, we believers must live in vital union with him. Our conduct must be consistent with this living relationship. People in the world should be able to see Christ by looking at Christians, seeing their values, lifestyles, and loving acts of service. The most important and effective way for believers to reflect Christ is by the way they relate to each other—being unified in devotion to God, loving one another as brothers and sisters in the faith (John 13:35) and as husband and wife (5:22-33), and using their gifts to encourage and build each other up (4:11-13).

What do people know about Jesus by watching how you relate to other Christians? In what ways can you use your God-given abilities to equip believers for service? Fulfill your role in the living church.

The new family (1:5; 2:11-19; 3:1-6; 4:1-6; 5:21-33). Because God through Christ paid the penalty for our sin and forgave us, we have been reconciled—brought near to him. We are a new society, a new family. Being united with Christ means that we are to treat one another as family members.

At one point, there was only one Son of God. But because God wanted a divine-human family, there are now many sons and daughters of God. As a consequence, Jesus Christ has many brothers and sisters. We are his family (2:19-20).

God's many sons and daughters compose his divine family (3:14-15). They are his inheritance and his glory (1:11, in the Greek; 2:19), for he has invested everything into them. He gave them his Son and created them anew in his Son. In the final day, when the time comes for God to display his glory to the whole universe (both visible and invisible), he will make a grand spectacle of all his children who, through transformation, will bear the image of Jesus Christ. God will be glorified, not just through Jesus Christ, but also through the church (3:10). His family is also his household and dwelling place. Those among whom he lives are also those in whom he lives (2:20-22).

Importance for today. Thank God that it was his good pleasure to include us in his Son, to impart to us—the believers—the divine, eternal life and to extend to us an opportunity to participate in the fellowship that he and his Son enjoyed from eternity. Because we are one family in Christ, we should have no barriers, division, or basis for discrimination. We all belong to Christ, so we should live in harmony with one another.

As a believer in Christ, you have a place where you are accepted and welcomed, where you belong—the church. You also have the responsibility to accept and welcome other believers, regardless of race, sex, occupation, nationality, ability, physical characteristics, social status, or personality type. And if you have a conflict with another believer, you should resolve the conflict as quickly as possible, maintaining unity and harmony.

How well do you relate to the other members of your Christian family? What can you do to help unify your church?

Christian conduct (2:1-10; 3:14-19; 4:1-3, 17-32; 5:1-33; 6:1-18). Ephesians encourages all Christians to wise, dynamic Christian living, for with privileges goes family responsibility. As a new community, we are to live by Christ's new standards.

God provides his Holy Spirit to enable us to live his way. The Holy Spirit, as the third person in the Trinity, is often described as God in action. When God moves and acts, he does so in and through the Spirit. Thus, everything that God accomplishes is by the Spirit. From the believers' perspective, then, all Christian activity must be done in and by the Spirit for it to be real. Thus, the Spirit is the medium through which God interacts with the church and the church interacts with God (2:18). This is why the church is called the "dwelling in which God lives by his Spirit" (2:22 NIV). Believers are called upon to live in the Spirit, to worship in the Spirit, to please the Spirit, and to maintain unity by the Spirit (4:3, 30; 5:9, 18-19). The church should display the full activity of the life-giving Spirit, or it is nothing more than a corpse.

Unfortunately, the Trinity and the church are not the only ones living in this universe; Satan and his host of wicked angels occupy the same realm. Their constant design is to ruin humanity and destroy the church—the object of all God's desires and designs. So there is constant warfare. Therefore, the church can't enjoy being just Christ's body and bride; it must also be Christ's warrior to stand against the attacks of Satan. Satan sees the church corporately. From his perspective, the church is a corporate warrior, armed with a full complement of divinely provided equipment. There is nothing that believers lack to fight against Satan. We have the belt of truth, the breastplate of righteousness, the shoes of the gospel, the shield of faith, the helmet of salvation, and the sword of the Spirit (6:12-18). With these we can defeat God's enemy.

Importance for today. Christians are under attack today as at no other time in history. Satan is working within the church to cause conflict and to divide, and he is moving against individuals, especially spiritual leaders, to prompt them to engage in self-centered sin. So we need all of our spiritual armor to win our spiritual battles. In addition to the armor, God gives us power through his Spirit. To utilize the Spirit's power, we must lay aside our evil desires and draw upon the power of his new life.

Are you ready for the battle? Do you know how to dress in your spiritual armor? Have you submitted your will to Christ?

VITAL STATISTICS

Purpose: To strengthen the believers in Ephesus in their Christian faith by explaining the nature and purpose of the church, the body of Christ

Author: Paul

To whom written: The church at Ephesus, and all believers everywhere

Date written: About A.D. 61, from Rome, during Paul's imprisonment there

Setting: The letter was not written to confront any heresy or problem in the churches. It was sent with Tychicus to strengthen and encourage the churches in the area. Paul had spent over three years with the Ephesian church. As a result, he was very close to them. Paul met with the elders of the Ephesian church at Miletus (Acts 20:17-38)—a meeting that was filled with great sadness because he was leaving them for what he thought would be the last time. Because there are no specific references to people or problems in the Ephesian church and because the words "at Ephesus" (1:1) are not present in some early manuscripts, Paul may have intended this to be a circular letter to be read to all the churches in the area.

Key verses: "There is one body and one Spirit—just as you were called to one hope when you were called—one Lord, one faith, one baptism; one God and Father of all, who is over all and through all and in all" (4:4-6 NIV).

OUTLINE

1. Unity in Christ (1:1–3:21)
2. Unity in the body of Christ (4:1–6:24)

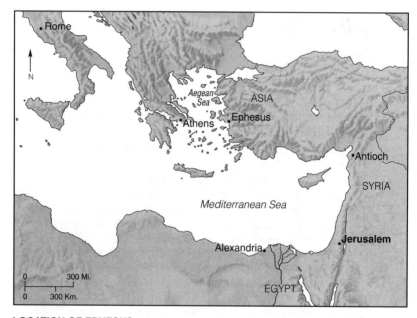

LOCATION OF EPHESUS
Ephesus was a strategic city, ranking in importance with Alexandria in Egypt and Antioch in Syria as a seaport. It lay on the most western edge of Asia Minor (modern-day Turkey), the most important port on the Aegean Sea on the main route from Rome to the East.

Ephesians 1

Paul wrote to the believers in Ephesus and the surrounding churches to give them in-depth teaching about how to nurture and maintain the unity of the church. He wanted to put this important information in written form because he was in prison for preaching the gospel and could not visit the churches himself.

Paul, writing in Greek, wrote one long sentence from 1:3 to 1:14 (which is not reflected in English translations). It forms the longest sentence ever found in ancient Greek. In this sentence, Paul introduced most of the themes he develops in this epistle. Paul used a technique rooted in Jewish worship known as the *berakah*—a form of praise. The language and style suggest influence by Hebrew psalms and hymns, which would have been significant to Paul in his spiritual upbringing. This one long sentence forms a eulogy, praising God for the blessings he has showered on believers because of his grace. These blessings come as a result of Christians' identification with Christ and the presence and work of the Holy Spirit in their lives. All of this occurred according to God's plan and purpose—his people were chosen in Christ "before the foundation of the world" (1:4 NKJV). Because it was God's plan, believers can trust that their salvation is certain—nothing can change what God has purposed. Because it was God's plan, believers also know that they were called and chosen for a purpose: to "be holy and without blame before Him in love" (1:4 NKJV) and that they "might live for the praise of his glory" (1:12 NRSV). Finally, because it was God's plan, Paul wanted his readers to understand God's ultimate purpose—"to bring all things in heaven and on earth together under one head, even Christ" (1:10 NIV). To be in Christ means to be part of God's plan for the redemption of sinful humanity in a sin-filled world—a plan he made before the earth was created! Believers are privileged to be chosen by God, saved by Christ, and filled with the Spirit, "who is a deposit guaranteeing our inheritance until the redemption of those who are God's possession—to the praise of his glory" (1:14 NIV). Through this eulogy, Paul demonstrated that believers have all spiritual blessings; then he prayed that they would know God intimately (1:17) in order that they might understand their *past* call to salvation, their *future* inheritance with Christ, and their *present* power available to them through the Spirit.

This eulogy serves to introduce Paul's letter by focusing the readers on their privileged position with God and the blessings he has heaped on them. From this beginning, Paul would teach them about unity in the church and about living as lights in their dark world.

1:1 Paul. Saul (whom we know as *Paul*) was a Jew from the tribe of Benjamin. He was raised as a strict Pharisee (Philippians 3:5), grew up in Tarsus, and was educated under a well-known teacher, Gamaliel (Acts 22:3). However, he was also a Roman citizen, a fact that he used to great advantage at times (Acts 22:27-29). Out of this diverse background, God formed and called a valuable servant, using every aspect of Paul's upbringing to further the gospel.

The Jewish name "Saul," given to a man born in the tribe of Benjamin, evoked memories of the tribe's days of glory. The first king of Israel was named Saul and came from this tribe (1 Samuel 10:20, 24-26). The Roman name "Paul" *(Paulus)* was a common surname (see, for example, Sergius Paulus in Acts 13:7). The name may have been a family name, or Paul may have chosen the name simply because of how close it sounded to his Jewish name. In Acts, Luke wrote, "Then Saul, who also is called Paul" (Acts 13:9 NKJV), and then used only the name "Paul" throughout the rest of the book. When Paul accepted the Christian faith and began his mission to the Gentiles, he identified with his listeners by using his Roman name. In all of his letters, Paul identified himself with his Roman name, linking himself with the Gentile believers to whom God had sent him with the gospel of Christ.

Following the style of first-century letters, Paul began his letter to the Ephesians, like all of his letters, by introducing himself as the writer. Paul used a scribe (secretary) for his letters (see Romans 16:22), dictating as the scribe wrote. Paul then often added the last few lines in his own hand to validate the document. Tertius served as Paul's scribe for Romans (Romans 16:22), as did other unnamed individuals (see 1 Corinthians 16:21; Galatians 6:11; Colossians 4:18; 2 Thessalonians 3:17). Paul also had people deliver these letters directly to the recipients. Tychicus probably carried this letter to the Ephesians (see 6:21-22) and may also have carried the letter to the Colossians (Colossians 4:7-9).

An apostle of Jesus Christ by the will of God.^{NKJV} Paul was an *apostle of Jesus Christ.* Paul was not one of the original twelve disciples (later called apostles), but the risen Christ Jesus confronted him on the road to Damascus and called him to preach the gospel to Jews and Gentiles (Acts 9:3-19). The apostles' mission was to be God's representatives: They were envoys, messengers, delegates, directly under the authority of Jesus Christ. They had authority to set up and supervise churches and to discipline them if necessary, which Paul did on all three of his missionary journeys and after his release from this first imprisonment in Rome.

In some letters (Galatians, for example), Paul called himself an apostle at the outset of the letter but then explained and defended his apostleship to that doubting congregation. The Ephesian church most likely had no doubt about Paul's authority as an apostle. However, Paul used the opening he commonly used in letters (see, for example, 2 Timothy 1:1) because this letter was to be circulated to other churches and congregations whom Paul had not met.

God chose Paul for special work, saying that Paul would be his "chosen instrument to take my message to the Gentiles and to kings, as well as to the people of Israel" (Acts 9:15 NLT). Paul did not seek this apostleship; instead, God chose him. Thus, Paul could truthfully say that he was an apostle *by the will of God* (see 1:1). God selected Paul for the apostleship through the same "will" that originated the church (1:5, 9, 11; Galatians 1:4).

BY THE WILL OF GOD
An apostle was a messenger, a "sent one." Paul says he was Jesus' messenger "by the will of God." If ever there was a clear-cut case of someone's not choosing God but being chosen *by* him, it was Paul of Tarsus. Saul, as he was then named, was a violent persecutor of the church. He was there when Stephen was martyred (Acts 7:58). He was heading to Damascus to do more harm to Christians when Jesus stopped him in his tracks. From that moment, Paul followed, later becoming Christianity's greatest missionary. Whatever sins you have committed, whatever shameful thoughts or deeds haunt your past—or present— they are minor compared to Paul's. If God's grace was sufficient for him, it is sufficient for you. Let go of your feelings of guilt or inadequacy, and leave them at the foot of the cross. Paul did, and the world has never been the same.

To the saints in Ephesus, the faithful in Christ Jesus.^{NIV} Paul wrote this letter to the Ephesian believers *(the saints in Ephesus).* The Bible uses "saints" to refer to three groups in the Bible:

angels, Israel, and the church (the body of believers). The word means "set apart ones." When Paul wrote to the saints in any area, he was referring to the believers there. These people were not "saints" because of any merit of their own; they were "saints" because they were set apart by God to devote themselves to the highest moral living. Paul emphasizes their dedication to God, not their personal holiness. (Of course, that personal holiness grew as they matured in their faith.) This is captured in Paul's greeting to the Roman believers: "To all in Rome who are loved by God and called to be saints" (Romans 1:7 NIV). Thus, the word "saint" denotes both the privilege and the responsibility of all true believers.

SAINTS AND STAINED GLASS
A little girl who attended worship in a place with a lot of stained-glass windows was asked what a saint was. "A saint is a person the light shines through," she replied. A saint is someone whose life—speech, actions, attitudes, relationships—points to Jesus. Does yours? The Bible teaches that *all* believers are saints—including you! This is not a reflection of your personal holiness but of the fact that a holy God has set you apart for his purposes. Face your day ready to treat each responsibility or each relationship as an opportunity to reflect God's mercy to others.

The words "in Ephesus" are not present in the three earliest manuscripts. Therefore, this was very likely a circular letter, meaning the name of each local church would be filled in as the letter circulated from church to church. Ephesus, the leading church in the region of Asia Minor, was probably the first destination for this epistle. Paul mentioned no particular problems or local situations, and he offered no personal greetings as he might have done if this letter were intended for the Ephesian church alone. (See, for example, his admonishing of the Galatian church in Galatians 3:1-5 and his personal greetings to people in the church at Philippi in Philippians 4:2-3.)

Ephesus was one of the five major cities in the Roman Empire, along with Rome, Corinth, Antioch, and Alexandria. Ephesus was a commercial, political, and religious center for all of Asia Minor. The population during the first century may have reached 250,000. The temple to the Greek goddess Artemis (Diana is her Roman equivalent) was located there. Paul first visited Ephesus at the end of his second missionary journey on his way back to Antioch (Acts 18:19-21). During his third missionary journey, he stayed there for almost three years (Acts 19; 20:31), obviously getting to know and love the believers there. The book of Acts records some of the events in Ephesus during Paul's ministries there:

- During his first short visit, "He himself went into the synagogue and reasoned with the Jews. When they asked him to spend more time with them, he declined. But as he left, he promised, 'I will come back if it is God's will'" (Acts 18:19-21 NIV). Obviously, God wanted Paul to return to Ephesus.
- Upon arriving for his three-year stay during his third missionary journey, Paul met twelve of John the Baptist's disciples. Paul explained the work of the Holy Spirit and baptized them in the name of the Lord Jesus (Acts 19:1-7).
- Paul spoke first in the synagogue for three months, but the Jews refused to believe. So Paul and his followers went to the lecture hall of Tyrannus where he spoke the word of the Lord daily for two years, to both Jews and Gentiles (Acts 19:9-10).
- "God gave Paul the power to do unusual miracles" (Acts 19:11 NLT), so that even those who practiced magic collected their magic books and had a huge public book-burning (Acts 19:11-20). (Magic in those days was a mixture of deception and spiritualism, not to be confused with entertainers or even gospel prestidigitators who perform "magic" for audiences today.)
- Just before Paul planned to move on to Macedonia and Achaia, a riot occurred in the city. Demetrius, a silversmith who made statues of the Greek goddess Artemis (Diana), was angry that Paul's preaching threatened his livelihood and that of his fellow shrine makers. (The more people who believed in Jesus, the less market existed for the idols.) Demetrius and the "silversmith union" managed to start a riot in the city, after which Paul immediately left for Macedonia (Acts 19:21–20:1).
- After his ministry in Macedonia, Paul wanted to get back to Jerusalem by the Day of Pentecost, so he began the coastal voyage around Asia, going south and east back to Judea. However, at a stopover in Miletus, Paul "sent a message to the elders of the church at Ephesus, asking them to come down to meet him" (Acts 20:17 NLT). His words to them, recorded in Acts 20:18-35, reveal the deep love, strong fellowship, and unbreakable unity that had grown between Paul and these believers. Paul had cared for them and loved them, even cried over their needs. They responded with love and care for him, and sorrow over his leaving: "When he had said this, he knelt down with all of them and prayed. They all wept as they embraced him and kissed him. What grieved them most was

his statement that they would never see his face again. Then they accompanied him to the ship" (Acts 20:36-38 NIV).

Clearly, Paul had a deep love for the church in Ephesus. His last words to the Ephesian elders focused on two items: (1) warning them about false teachers: "I know full well that false teachers, like vicious wolves, will come in among you after I leave, not sparing the flock. Even some of you will distort the truth in order to draw a following. Watch out!" (Acts 20:29-31 NLT), and (2) exhorting them to show love and care toward one another: "Help the poor by working hard. You should remember the words of the Lord Jesus: 'It is more blessed to give than to receive'" (Acts 20:35 NLT).

Paul apparently received reports that the Ephesian church held up well against false teachers (see discussion on 4:14). However, perhaps the love, care, and unity Paul had called for were lacking. Thus, this letter speaks much of love and unity and the out-workings of these in relationships in the home and in the church. Paul knew that such teaching was needed not only in Ephesus but in every church—again pointing to the probable circular nature of this letter. Indeed, Paul's words applied in Ephesus and in all the Asian churches—and they apply to our churches today.

Paul also referred to the believers in Ephesus as *the faithful in Christ Jesus.* As opposed to the church in Galatia, which had, for a time, turned away from the faith, Paul commended these believers for remaining faithful and rejecting false teaching.

While these believers were "in Ephesus" (or in neighboring congregations), all believers are "in Christ Jesus." Jesus Christ brought a new relationship between God and people—we have a relationship with God only because of Christ Jesus and only because we are "in" him through our belief in him. In fact, Paul used this phrase (or a variation of it) twelve times in the first fourteen verses as he stressed the unity all believers should have because of their common bond in Christ. Not only do believers have faith, they are also faithful; however, it is only when believers are "in Christ Jesus" that they can be faithful. Faithfulness is possible only in Christ.

O COME, ALL YE FAITHFUL
"Faithful in Christ Jesus"—what an excellent reputation! Such a label would be an honor for any believer. What would it take for others to characterize you as faithful to Christ Jesus? Hold fast to your faith, one day at a time; faithfully obey God, even in the details of life. Then, like the Ephesians, you will be known as a person who is faithful to the Lord.

1:2 Grace to you and peace from God our Father and the Lord Jesus Christ.^{NKJV} "Grace" means God's undeserved favor. It is through God's kindness alone that anyone can become acceptable to God. As Paul will write later in this letter, "For by grace you have been saved through faith, and that not of yourselves; it is the gift of God" (2:8 NKJV).

"Peace" refers to the peace that Christ established between believers and God through his death on the cross. True peace is available only in Christ. Jesus said, "Peace I leave with you; my peace I give you. I do not give to you as the world gives. Do not let your hearts be troubled and do not be afraid" (John 14:27 NIV).

> Grace means the free, unmerited, unexpected love of God, and all the benefits, delights, and comforts which flow from it. It means that while we were sinners and enemies we have been treated as sons and heirs.
>
> *R. P. C. Hanson*

Paul used "grace and peace" as a standard greeting in all of his letters (see, for example, Romans 1:7; 1 Corinthians 1:3; 2 Corinthians 1:2; Galatians 1:3). He wanted his readers to experience God's grace and peace in their daily living. In these two words, Paul combined expressions from Jewish and Gentile customs. Jews wished one another "peace" *(eirene* or the Hebrew *shalom)*; Gentiles wished each other "grace" *(charis).* Already Paul was underscoring the unity of all believers—Jews and Gentiles alike—by using greetings common to both groups.

Only *God our Father and the Lord Jesus Christ* can grant such wonderful gifts. By mentioning "the Lord Jesus Christ" along with "God our Father," Paul was pointing to Jesus as a full person of the Godhead. He recognized Jesus' deity and lordship over all of creation. Both God the Father and Jesus Christ the Lord are coequal in providing the resources of grace and mercy.

1:3 Blessed be the God and Father of our Lord Jesus Christ, who has blessed us with every spiritual blessing in the heavenly places in Christ.^{NKJV} Here begins a lengthy passage that praises God for what he has done for us in Jesus Christ. This complex sentence is very difficult to analyze. Paul heaped praise upon praise, one thought leading into another, which then would remind him of another. This section forms a blessing, in Hebrew called a *berakah,* frequently used in Jewish liturgy. It is a eulogy for God and for all the blessings he gives his people.

In this prologue to the book, Paul summarizes the Trinity's plan for the church:

1. the *Father's* work of love in choosing us to holiness (1:4), sonship (1:5), and acceptance (1:6), to receive the knowledge of his will (1:8-9), to participate in his heading up all things in Christ (1:10), to be his inheritance (1:11), and to be his glory (1:12);
2. the *Son's* act of saving us (1:7) and being the head of all creation (1:10);
3. the *Holy Spirit's* work of making us secure (1:13) and becoming the guarantee of our eternal inheritance (1:14).

Paul first praised God, saying that God was to be *blessed.* The Greek word *eulogetos* comes from a verb meaning "to speak well of." It is an Old Testament benediction meaning "praise" (when people "bless" God). To say "blessed" be God, we are "blessing" God by recognizing and attributing worth to him. It is a word of praise and reverence. In the New Testament, this particular word, translated both "blessed" and "praise," is used only when speaking of God (see also Mark 14:61; Luke 1:68; Romans 1:25; 9:5; 2 Corinthians 1:3; 11:31; 1 Peter 1:3). God alone is worthy of our praise and our worship; he alone is worthy to be "blessed."

As believers know already, this praise and blessing is to be directed toward *the God and Father of our Lord Jesus Christ.* Paul may have been pointing out the essential unity of God and Christ, the unity believers have with both God and Christ, and thus, the unity believers ought to have with one another. (For similar wording, see also Romans 15:6; 1 Peter 1:3; Revelation 1:6.)

Then Paul gave the reason why God is worthy to be blessed: because he *has blessed us.* This verb means "to benefit, to prosper, to give contentment." This verb occurs hundreds of times in the Old Testament, revealing that God enjoys blessing his people. Here Paul used the past tense ("has blessed"), indicating that this prospering of believers had already occurred—even from eternity past. God has blessed us by allowing us to receive the benefits of Christ's redemption (1:7) and resurrection (1:19-20). God blessed us through Christ's death on the cross on our behalf.

In Christ, believers have *every spiritual blessing.* The phrase "in Christ" or its equivalent occurs twelve times in these verses. The same phrase occurs throughout the New Testament. Here it conveys the meaning of what God does for us through Christ, as well as depicts our unity with Christ. It shows the unique benefits given to us by Christ's work (see Romans 3:24; 6:23) but focuses on what will come to pass at the consummation of history when Christ rules in the new heaven and new earth. Because by faith we are under Christ's lordship, we have "every spiritual blessing"—that is, every benefit of knowing God and everything we need to grow spiritually. These are spiritual blessings, not material ones. Because God

OUR TRUE IDENTITY IN CHRIST

Romans 3:24	We are justified (declared "not guilty" of sin).
Romans 8:1	We await no condemnation.
Romans 8:2	We are set free from the law of sin and death.
1 Corinthians 1:2	We are sanctified and made acceptable in Jesus Christ.
1 Corinthians 1:30	We are righteous and holy in Christ.
1 Corinthians 15:22	We will be made alive at the Resurrection.
2 Corinthians 5:17	We are a new creation.
2 Corinthians 5:21	We receive God's righteousness.
Galatians 3:28	We are one in Christ with all other believers.
Ephesians 1:3	We are blessed with every spiritual blessing in Christ.
Ephesians 1:4	We are holy, blameless, and the objects of God's love.
Ephesians 1:5-6	We are adopted as God's children.
Ephesians 1:7	We are forgiven—our sins are taken away.
Ephesians 1:10-11	We will be brought under Christ's headship.
Ephesians 1:13	We are marked as belonging to God by the Holy Spirit.
Ephesians 2:6	We have been raised up to sit with Christ in glory.
Ephesians 2:10	We are God's work of art.
Ephesians 2:13	We have been brought near to God.
Ephesians 3:6	We share in the promises of the gospel.
Ephesians 3:12	We can come with freedom and confidence into God's presence.
Ephesians 5:29-30	We are members of Christ's body, the church.
Colossians 2:10	We have been given fullness in Christ.
Colossians 2:11	We are set free from our sinful nature.
2 Timothy 2:10	We will have eternal glory.

has already blessed believers, we need not ask for these blessings but simply accept them and apply them to our lives. Because we have an intimate relationship with Christ, we can enjoy these blessings now and will enjoy them for eternity.

The phrase *heavenly places* occurs five times in this letter:

1. Believers are blessed with every spiritual blessing in the "heavenly places" (1:3).
2. Christ is seated at God's right hand in the "heavenly places" (1:20).
3. We have been raised up to sit with Christ in the "heavenly places" (2:6).
4. God is being made known to the rulers and authorities in the "heavenly places" (3:10).
5. We struggle against the spiritual forces of evil in the "heavenly places" (6:12).

When Paul refers to the "heavenly places," he refers to the
sphere beyond the material world—the place of spiritual activity
where the ultimate conflict between good and evil takes place.
This conflict continues but has already been won by Christ's
death and resurrection. This is the realm in which the spiritual
blessings were secured for us and then given to us. Our blessings
come from heaven, where Christ now lives (1:20), and Christ's
gift of the Holy Spirit, the source of all spiritual blessings, came
as a result of his ascension to heaven (4:8). Paul was making the
point that these blessings are spiritual and not material; thus, they
are eternal and not temporal. Oddly enough, while this phrase is
used five times in this letter, it is found in none of Paul's other letters. Although the phrase is not used elsewhere, the thought is.
Read these other quotations from Paul:

- *So we don't look at the troubles we can see right now; rather,*
  we look forward to what we have not yet seen. For the troubles
  we see will soon be over, but the joys to come will last forever.
  (2 Corinthians 4:18 NLT*)*

- *Since, then, you have been raised with Christ, set your hearts*
  on things above, where Christ is seated at the right hand of
  God. Set your minds on things above, not on earthly things.
  For you died, and your life is now hidden with Christ in God.
  When Christ, who is your life, appears, then you also will
  appear with him in glory. (Colossians 3:1-4 NIV*)*

IN CHRIST
Although you have the blessing of a special relationship with
Christ, do you sometimes experience the tension of being a
Christian in a non-Christian world? It's like having one foot
on a dock and one foot in a boat leaving the dock. Jesus
acknowledged this when he prayed for us in John 17, saying
that we would be *in* the world and yet not *of* it. The reason we
experience this struggle is that we are "in Christ" (we have a
relationship with him). Formerly we were "in Adam" (according
to Romans 5, unbelievers are totally identified with Adam's sin);
we were fallen, thoroughly stained and twisted by sin, unable
to please God. But now, by God's grace, we who believe are "in
Christ": still fallen, still sin-scarred, but now we are made right
with God through faith. When the pressure and temptation of
the non-Christian world seem too strong, don't be surprised
and don't be discouraged. God has begun a new work in you,
reversing the effects of the Fall and restoring you to what you
were intended to be, a new person—"in Christ." Keep him as
the Lord of your life.

**1:4 For he chose us in him before the creation of the world to be
holy and blameless in his sight. In love . . .**[NIV] Verses 3 and 4
are one continuous sentence, meaning that believers are blessed
in Christ with every spiritual blessing because God chose us in
Christ. We have these blessings because of God's choosing us
(1:4), Christ's dying for us (1:7), and the Holy Spirit's sealing us
(1:13). God gives spiritual blessings to believers because of the
saving work of all three persons in the Trinity.

That God *chose us* forms the basis of
the doctrine of election—defined as
God's choice of an individual or group
for a specific purpose or destiny. The
doctrine of election teaches that we are
saved only because of God's grace and
mercy; as believers we are not saved by
our own merit. It focuses on God's purpose or will (1:5, 9, 11), not on ours. God
does not save us because we deserve it
but because he graciously and freely
gives salvation. We did not influence
God's decision to save us; he saved us
according to his plan. Thus, we may not
take credit for our salvation or take pride in our wise choice.

> Salvation is from our
> side a choice, from the
> divine side it is a seizing
> upon, an apprehending,
> a conquest by the
> Most High God. Our
> "accepting" and "willing"
> are reactions rather than
> actions. The right of
> determination must
> always remain with God.
> *A. W. Tozer*

The doctrine of election runs through the Bible, beginning with
God's choosing Abraham's descendants as his special people.
Through them, God would fulfill his promise to Abraham that "in
you all the families of the earth shall be blessed" (Genesis 12:3
NKJV). Listen to the words of Moses:

■ *For you are a people holy to the* LORD *your God. The* LORD
*your God has chosen you out of all the peoples on the face of
the earth to be his people, his treasured possession. The* LORD
*did not set his affection on you and choose you because you
were more numerous than other peoples, for you were the few-
est of all peoples. But it was because the* LORD *loved you and
kept the oath he swore to your forefathers that he brought you
out with a mighty hand and redeemed you from the land of slavery, from the power of Pharaoh king of Egypt. . . . Therefore,
take care to follow the commands, decrees and laws I give you
today. (Deuteronomy 7:6-8, 11* NIV*)*

Israel fulfilled a specific purpose: it was the nation into whom
the Savior, Jesus Christ, was born as a human being. "Election"
connotes special status, building on its use in the Old Testament

to define Israel as the special people of God who inherit the land, receive his Word, and then convey that Word to all the nations.

The nation did not follow the commandments Moses gave them from God, however, so they wound up in exile because of their sins. After the nation went into exile, the prophets told the people that God had chosen a "remnant" (a small group) of true believers who would remain after the Exile (see, for example, Isaiah 10:20-22; 37:31-32; Jeremiah 42:2; Micah 2:12; 5:7-8; Zephaniah 3:12-13; Haggai 1:14; Zechariah 8:6, 12).

Even many among this remnant of Jews eventually turned away. Although the Jews were chosen as special recipients and emissaries of God's grace, their opportunity to participate in that plan arrived with the coming of Christ, their promised Messiah. But many didn't recognize Christ and so rejected him. As John wrote: "He came to that which was his own, but his own did not receive him. Yet to all who received him, to those who believed in his name, he gave the right to become children of God—children born not of natural descent, nor of human decision or a husband's will, but born of God" (John 1:11-13 NIV). The "all who received" Jesus included Jews and Gentiles alike. Thus, God's "chosen" and elected people are now Christians, the body of Christ, the church— all who believe on, accept, and receive Jesus Christ as Messiah, Savior, and Lord. Jesus himself called his followers "the elect" (see Matthew 24:22, 24, 31; Mark 13:20, 22, 27). Paul called the believers "a remnant, chosen by grace" (Romans 11:5 NRSV).

WHY ME?
Why would God choose some and not others? A better question is, Why would God choose anyone at all? We will never fully plumb the depths of God's purposes in election, but Ephesians 1:4 gives some insight into them. We are to be "holy and blameless" before him. When we select members of a sports team for awards, we look for those most capable, desirable, and worthy. Not so with God; he seems to delight in choosing the most unlikely. And in calling us "before the creation of the world"—before we had done anything to demonstrate our own worthiness or lack thereof—God shows that his decision has nothing to do with our righteousness, and everything to do with his compassion. When your head spins with the mystery of election, let your heart also swell with the reality of grace.

In Ephesians 1:4-5, Paul gave four specific components of this election: (1) It is "in him" (in Christ, because of his sacrifice on our behalf); (2) it is "before the creation of the world" (from

eternity past); (3) it is done for a specific purpose: "to be holy
and blameless in his sight"; and (4) it is an act of "love." Our
salvation rests on God's choosing us. Our being chosen rests on
God's love and mercy alone. Therefore, salvation is completely
certain, and it is eternal. Believers are chosen *in him* (in Christ).
This parallels the words in verse 3. We are blessed in Christ and
we are chosen in Christ, again emphasizing the spiritual sphere of
this election by God. In addition, we have blessings and election
only because of what Christ has done for us.

The mystery of salvation originated in the timeless mind of
God long *before the creation of the world* (see 2 Thessalonians
2:13; 2 Timothy 1:9). Before God created anything, his plan was
in place to give eternal salvation to those who would believe on
his Son. Before God created people, he knew sin would occur, he
knew a penalty would have to be paid, and he knew that he himself (in his Son) would pay it.

What God began in eternity past will be completed in eternity
future. God's purpose in choosing us was that we would *be holy
and blameless.* Believers are chosen not just to be saved but also
to live changed lives during their remaining time on earth. To be
"holy" means to be set apart for God in order to reflect his nature.
We are chosen by God for a new life, new goals, and a certain
future in eternity with him. As Paul wrote to the Romans, "For
those God foreknew he also predestined to be conformed to the
likeness of his Son, that he might be the firstborn among many
brothers" (Romans 8:29 NIV). We are set apart, and we are to live
blamelessly—without fault, blemish, or defect (see also Philippians
2:15). The Old Testament used "blameless" to refer to animals
acceptable for sacrifice to God (see Leviticus 1:3, 10). Christ
offered himself as a sacrifice on our behalf—he "offered himself
unblemished to God" for a purpose: "that we may serve the living
God!" (Hebrews 9:14 NIV). (See note on 5:27.)

It may seem difficult to understand how God could accept
anyone. But because of Christ, believers are made *holy and
blameless* in God's sight. God chose us, and when we belong to
him through Jesus Christ, God looks at us as though we had
never sinned. Our appropriate responses are love, worship, and
service—in thankfulness for his wonderful grace. We must never
take our privileged status as a license for sin.

Paul wrote that we are holy and without blame *in his sight.*
That is, we have received the awesome privilege of standing in
God's presence. Every act we do is *in his sight,* for God knows us
thoroughly. "In his sight" means in his perfect moral judgment.
The image is not so much of an all-seeing eye as of a judge who

pardons because, in his judgment, there are no longer charges against the accused. Paul knew and testified to the truth that God knew all his thoughts, actions, and motives (see Romans 1:9; 2 Corinthians 4:2; Galatians 1:20; 1 Thessalonians 2:5). So with every believer. We cannot hide from God. Thankfully, while God sees and knows us completely, he also sees us as he has made us and will perfect us. And when we at last stand before God the Judge, we know that God will accept us because of Christ's sacrifice (Colossians 1:22; Revelation 7:14).

To which clause do the words "in love" attach? To verse 4, "holy and without blame before him in love," or to verse 5, "in love he predestined us"? Most likely, the words "in love" modify the words following it (thus tying into verse 5), pointing out that God's love is shown in predestination. The fact that God chooses and predestines believers for a glorious future with him is most certainly an act of love. Love is both the basis for and the end product of our holiness.

1:5 **He predestined us to be adopted as his sons through Jesus Christ, in accordance with his pleasure and will.**^NIV "Predestined" comes from the Greek word *proorisas* meaning "marked out beforehand." Being "chosen" and being "predestined" are God's work and not our own doing. The "predestined" people (those chosen, elected) become God's children through a process Paul compares to adoption.

ADOPTION
Our relationship with God is like one in which a judge "throws the book" at a lawbreaker and then comes out from behind the bench and pays the penalty for the guilty one. Yet that analogy doesn't go far enough. According to Ephesians 1:5, the judge not only pays the penalty, but he then takes the offender home and adopts him or her into his family. *What amazing compassion!* We stand guilty as charged and convicted before God, the righteous Judge. But thanks to the atoning sacrifice of Jesus, we are "pardoned"—declared not guilty—and set free. Even more, we are taken into God's family and given the status of sons and daughters. When you consider your standing before God, do you see yourself as a pardoned convict or as an adopted child? Devote your life to fulfilling God's purposes and show your true status as his child.

In his infinite love, God chose for us *to be adopted* as his own children. People were created to have fellowship with God (Genesis 1:26), but because of their sin, they forfeited that fellowship. Through Jesus' sacrifice, God brought us back into his family and made us heirs along with Jesus (Romans 8:17). God did not do this as an emergency measure after sin engulfed creation; instead, God knew from the beginning this would happen. People were "predestined" to be "adopted." Under Roman law, adopted children had the same rights and privileges as biological children. Even if they had been slaves, adopted children became full heirs in their new family. Paul used this term to show the strength and permanence of believers' relationship to God. This adoption occurs *through Jesus Christ,* for only his sacrifice on our behalf enables us to receive what God intended for us.

Not only had God planned this from the beginning, but he also planned it *in accordance with his pleasure and will.* The Greek word translated "pleasure" *(eudokia)* can mean a good feeling one person has toward another, or, where there is no object, this "pleasure" can be translated as "purpose" (see also 1:9). The word for "will" in Greek conveys more emotion than volition; God's will, therefore, means God's heart's desire. Predestination, election, and adoption are all part of God's purpose and God's will, a magnificent expression of God's character.

CHOSEN IN HIM
Very few issues cause more confusion and even arguments among Christians than the issues of election and predestination. It is very difficult to simultaneously embrace God's sovereignty and human responsibility. Election was not a theological concept dreamed up by Paul; it appears throughout Scripture. Even though we may not be able to completely comprehend how these two truths can coexist, we can say this:

Election . . .
- comes from the heart of God, not the mind of people;
- should be an incentive to please God, not to ignore him;
- should give birth to gratitude, not complacency.

Human responsibility . . .
- requires that we actively confess Christ as Lord;
- focuses on living according to God's plan;
- requires that we share the gospel with everyone.

Election energizes a Christian's life of obedient service. Responsibility challenges us to build a life "worthy of the calling" we have received (Ephesians 4:1). As you consider God's divine selection of you, how do you respond—with pride or apathy, or with a worshipful heart and obedience?

1:6 To the praise of his glorious grace, which he has freely given us in the One he loves.^NIV God's goal in the election of believers was that they would praise him. Therefore, the ultimate purpose of believers' lives is to praise God because of his merciful dealings with us, shown in 1:3, 6, 12, 14. We praise him first for *his glorious grace.* His *grace* (the unmerited favor he shows his chosen ones) is indeed *glorious*—without it, we would have no hope, and our lives would be nothing more than a few years on earth. Instead, we have purpose for living and hope of eternal life.

His grace was *freely given.* It was a free gift, not something we could earn or deserve. The means of this grace giving is indicated in the last phrase, *in the One he loves.* God's grace was given flesh and blood—we could "see" it—when Jesus Christ came to earth and died for our sins. God graciously accepts us (though we don't deserve it) now that we belong to his dearly loved Son. God's favor to us is realized by our union with Christ. We could say that God's love for his only Son motivated him to have many more sons— each of whom would be like his Son (Romans 8:28-30) by being in his Son and by being conformed to his image.

TO THE PRAISE OF HIS GLORIOUS GRACE
Praise means celebrating God. Undoubtedly you have seen, and probably participated in, celebrations like Fourth of July fireworks displays and Memorial Day parades. The purpose of such festivities is not simply to set off firecrackers and Roman candles or to watch graying veterans march down city streets. The events are held to remember and honor the sacrifices of men and women who went before and paid the price for freedom. As Christians, our lives are living tributes to God's grace. God selected us as believers so that we might praise him. When others look at our lives, what kinds of "tributes" do they see? Liberated, engaging individuals, full of gratitude for all he has done for us? Or shrivelled, sullen, embittered shells that feel as though we've been cheated out of life's good things? Let your prayer life and worship express your gratitude to God.

The reference to Jesus Christ (also called the "Beloved" in other translations) gives a transition from election to God's redemptive act in accomplishing that election and adoption through his Son, Jesus Christ. Paul poured forth a litany of praise for this second person of the Trinity.

1:7-8 In him we have redemption through his blood, the forgive- ness of sins.^NIV "In him" refers directly back to the last words of verse 6—"the One [God] loves," that is, Jesus Christ. It is in Jesus Christ alone that *we have redemption,* for it is when we believe in Jesus Christ as Savior that we are redeemed. "Redemp- tion" refers to Christ's setting sinners free from slavery to sin. In

Old Testament times, the word referred to a person's being freed from slavery or from prison (Leviticus 25:47-54). To redeem this person involved paying a price, sometimes called a "ransom." It meant buying that person's freedom. Jesus provides a sinner's full redemption. Believers are "justified freely by his grace through the redemption that came by Christ Jesus" (Romans 3:24 NIV). Thus, Paul can confidently praise Jesus by saying that *in him we have redemption.* This includes release from the guilt and the deserved punishment for sin. Christ became human, like us, so that he could free us from slavery to sin.

SET FREE!
Christ has bought us back from the tyranny of sin—literally "ransomed" us. At a terrible price: his life. He has set us free from those enemies that once owned us—fear, prejudice, lust, anger, legalism, greed—and made us his own. Imagine you are a slave and you belong to a horrible master who has no regard for your health, your feelings, or your life in general. One day a benevolent stranger buys you at a staggering price and sets you free—completely free. How would you respond? Would you show appreciation for your liberator? sing his praises to anyone who would listen? Would you ever willingly go back to your degrading bondage? Your life should reflect gratitude for what Christ has done. Don't return to your former bondage. Claim your freedom in Christ!

Paul's use of the present tense ("we have") indicates a present and continous reality that the Ephesian believers already possessed. Redemption is a present reality—not past tense, "you were redeemed at one time but have to keep being redeemed"; not future tense, "someday you'll be redeemed." (Besides the present reality, the word "redemption" also has an eschatological usage referring to believers' future inheritance and hope—see examples of that usage in 1:14 and 4:30.)

All people are enslaved to sin. Jesus paid the price to redeem us, to buy our freedom from sin. The purchase price was *his blood.* To speak of Jesus' blood was an important first-century way of speaking of Christ's death. Our redemption was costly— Jesus paid the price with his life. Through his death, Jesus released us from slavery to sin and gave us *forgiveness of sins.* When we believe, an exchange takes place. We give Christ our sins, and he gives us redemption and forgiveness. Our sin was poured into Christ at his crucifixion. His righteousness was poured into us at our conversion. God's forgiveness means that

GOD'S RICHES GIVEN TO US

God is rich in kindness, tolerance, and patience. . . . . . . Romans 2:4

God makes known the riches of his glory. . . . . Romans 9:23

God is rich in wisdom and knowledge. . . . . Romans 11:33

Though Christ was rich, he became poor for the
    sake of sinners, so that through his poverty, we
    might be made rich. . . . . 2 Corinthians 8:9

Believers' redemption and forgiveness are part of
    the riches of God's grace. . . . . Ephesians 1:7

Paul prayed that the believers would know
    the riches of their inheritance. . . . . Ephesians 1:18

God is rich in mercy. . . . . Ephesians 2:4

The riches of God's grace are incomparable. . . . . Ephesians 2:7

Paul was called to preach to the Gentiles the
    unsearchable riches of Christ. . . . . Ephesians 3:8

Paul prayed that God would strengthen the believers
    out of his glorious riches. . . . . Ephesians 3:16

Paul said that God would grant the believers'
    needs according to his glorious riches. . . . . Philippians 4:19

God is making known the riches of this mystery—
    Christ in the believers. . . . . Colossians 1:27

Paul wanted the believers to have the full riches
    of complete understanding in order to know the
    mystery of Christ's work in people. . . . . Colossians 2:2

---

he no longer even remembers believers' past sins. We are completely forgiven.

The word "sins" here is *paraptoma*. It refers to sinful acts, straying from the right path, the daily actions that betray our sin nature. God's forgiveness deals with both our sin nature *and* our daily sins. To doubt this, or to think that one's sins are too bad to be forgiven, is to doubt the value of Christ's sacrifice. He shed his blood for you. All sins can be covered with his blood.

But why blood? Why did our redemption and forgiveness have to come through Jesus' death? God made it clear that "without the shedding of blood there is no forgiveness" (Hebrews 9:22 NIV). Forgiveness of sins was granted in Old Testament times on the basis of the shedding of animals' blood (Leviticus 17:11). At the time of their exodus from Egypt, the Israelites were spared from the plague of death by killing a lamb

> God commands us to be filled with the Spirit; and if we aren't filled, it's because we're living beneath our privileges.
>
> *D. L. Moody*

with no defects and then placing the blood on the doorframes of their homes. In killing the lamb, the Israelites shed innocent blood. The lamb was a sacrifice, a substitute for the person who would have died that night. In spiritual terms, in order for sinful people to be spared, an innocent life had to be sacrificed in their place. Animal sacrifices constantly reminded people of their sin and its penalty.

How, then, does blood make atonement for sin? The Old Testament believers symbolically transferred their sins to an animal, which they then sacrificed (see a description of this ceremony in Leviticus 4). The animal died in their place to pay for their sin and to allow them to continue living in God's favor. God graciously forgave them because of their faith in him and because they obeyed his commandments concerning the sacrifice. Those sacrifices anticipated the day when Christ would completely remove sin. Real cleansing from sin came with Jesus, the "Lamb of God, who takes away the sin of the world" (John 1:29 NIV). Sin, by its very nature, brings death— that is a fact as certain as the law of gravity. Jesus did not die for his own sins; he had none. Instead, by a transaction that we can never fully understand, he died for the sins of the world. This sacrifice was necessary in order to satisfy God's justice. He will not just forgive sins without price; a penalty for sin had to be paid. But in his love he chose to pay the penalty in his Son. When believers commit their lives to Christ and thus iden-tify themselves with him, his death becomes theirs. He has paid the penalty for sins, and his blood has purified all those who believe in him. (See also Romans 5:9; Ephesians 2:13; Colossians 1:20.)

Jesus became the final and ultimate sacrifice for sin. Instead of an unblemished lamb slain on the altar, the perfect Lamb of God was slain on the cross, a sinless sacrifice so that our sins could be forgiven once and for all. "For you know that it was not with per-ishable things such as silver or gold that you were redeemed . . . but with the precious blood of Christ, a lamb without blemish or defect" (1 Peter 1:18-19 NIV). All who believe in Christ receive redemption and forgiveness.

In accordance with the riches of God's grace that he lavished on us with all wisdom and understanding.NIV Our redemption and forgiveness are *in accordance with the riches of God's grace.* The ultimate sacrifice, Jesus, bought our redemption and forgive-ness. As astounding as that is, it is "in accordance" with God's riches; that is, God's grace is an expression of his munificence.

God's redemption, forgiveness, and grace to us are infinite, eternal, unchanging, and far beyond our understanding.

Paul referred to God's "riches" six times in this letter. He also used the word in other letters to explain the infinite and priceless nature of God's character and actions toward people. (See the chart, "God's Riches Given to Us.")

GRACE
A good definition of "grace" is "God doing for us that which we do not deserve and could not do for ourselves." Religion is often defined in terms of "people's efforts to reach God." Virtually all religions have moral and ethical principles—a framework for judging right from wrong. "Do these things, don't do those things, and you may attain God's blessings or maybe even become God yourself." That is the basic message of the world's great religions . . . except one. Christianity *does* have a set of moral and ethical principles, to be sure; there are ten recorded in Exodus 20 for starters. But the message of Christianity is that you can never *do* enough good deeds or *avoid* enough bad deeds to reach God. God has to reach you— and that is what he did in the person of Jesus of Nazareth. Are you trying to get to God through your own efforts? Why live in poverty? Make use of his storehouses of kindness and grace for you.

God's "grace" means his unmerited favor. Only by God's grace is anyone redeemed and forgiven. Paul here used his characteristic word "riches" to picture the value of this grace. People can do nothing to be saved; God's grace alone allows it to happen. It was God's grace alone that sent Christ to accomplish our redemption. We owe our lives—present and eternal—to the riches of God's grace. Not only was this grace given, it also was *lavished on us,* generously showered on us. God wants to give grace to people, and when he gives, he gives abundantly and extravagantly. Paul's language expressed joy—the riches are bountiful or infinite and are meant for us, his people.

In the phrase "with all wisdom and understanding," the word "wisdom" *(sophia)* is the ability to see life from God's perspective. Proverbs 9:10 teaches that the fear (respect and honor) of the Lord is the beginning of wisdom. The word "understanding" *(phronesis)* could also be translated "insight," referring to the ability to discern the right action to take in any given situation. Wisdom and understanding are given to believers for them to know God's will. It is certainly true that to understand God's will, people need wisdom and understanding from God. It could also be true that it was God's perfect wisdom to allow the revelation to be seen by the apostle and then by all believers.

1:9 And he made known to us the mystery of his will according to his good pleasure, which he purposed in Christ.^{NIV} Paul had been praising God's wonderful grace in 1:7-8. Thoughts of grace led Paul to praise God for the entire plan of salvation—what had been seen and what would yet be revealed. God had purposed to offer salvation to humanity "before the foundation of the world" (1:4). How this would happen was not *made known* (made clear, revealed, understood) until the death and resurrection of Jesus Christ.

What God "made known" was his plan to bring people (both Jews and Gentiles) back into fellowship with himself through their faith in Christ and then to keep them with him for all eternity. Paul called this *the mystery of his will . . . which he purposed in Christ.* Paul used the word "mystery" several times in this letter (see 3:3, 4, 9; 5:32; 6:19; see also Romans 11:25; Colossians 1:26-27; 2:2; 4:3). It has two meanings in Hellenistic Greek. One meaning referred to something secret and known to only a select few. The word described heathen religions or "mystery religions" with their secret rites and practices. As used in the Septuagint (a Greek version of the Jewish Old Testament writings), a second meaning of the word describes what God reveals (as in Daniel 2:19). The Jews used the word to describe some secret plan that God would reveal at the end of the age. In the New Testament, the word refers to a truth formerly hidden but now made known to people—in this case, *to us,* meaning all believers. In Colossians 1:26-27, it refers to Christ's decisive action here and now. In this verse, it refers to God's plan to unite all things in heaven and earth in Christ.

It was God's "will" from the beginning to give his people glorious privileges. The fact that Paul ties the word "mystery" in with "God's will" reveals the certainty of the outcome of God's plans and promises. As with our election (1:4), so the revelation of the mystery of salvation is *according to his good pleasure.* It pleases God to make known to us the mystery of his will.

1:10 To be put into effect when the times will have reached their fulfillment—to bring all things in heaven and on earth together under one head, even Christ.^{NIV} The Greek word *oikonomia* (translated here "to be put into effect") refers to the management of a household or estate. In this context, it refers to large-scale management, as in administration or economy. Christ will put everything into effect according to God's timing. "God was pleased to have all his fullness dwell in [Christ], and through him to reconcile to himself all things, whether things on earth or things in heaven, by making peace through his blood, shed on the cross" (Colossians 1:19-20 NIV).

With his first coming, Christ completed part of this mystery. "When the time had fully come, God sent his Son . . ." (Galatians 4:4 NIV). But there are promises yet to be fulfilled. The mystery of salvation does not end with a person's acceptance of Jesus Christ—God promises a glorious future in a glorious kingdom (see Revelation 21–22). This time is unknown to everyone but God.

The "times" to which Paul referred were not the passage of time, as in days and months (that Greek word is *chronos*). Instead, Paul used the word *kairos,* referring here to the "end times," and those "times" are God's alone. The conversion of the Jews, Christ's return, and the new heaven and earth are other specific "times" that will occur in the future when it pleases God.

At that time, God is planning *to bring all things in heaven and on earth together under one head, even Christ.* God is planning a universal reconciliation—all of creation will be reinstated to its rightful owner and creator—Christ. Just as Christ administered God's plan of redemption by carrying it out as a human on this earth, so he will ultimately be in charge of "all things in heaven and on earth." All of creation (spiritual and material) will be brought back under one head:

- All of heaven. "All the angels were standing around the throne and around the elders and the four living creatures. They fell down on their faces before the throne and worshiped God." (Revelation 7:11 NIV)
- All people. "That at the name of Jesus every knee should bow, of those in heaven, and of those on earth, and of those under the earth, and that every tongue should confess that Jesus Christ is Lord." (Philippians 2:10-11 NKJV)
- All creation itself. "For the creation was subjected to frustration, not by its own choice, but by the will of the one who subjected it, in hope that the creation itself will be liberated from its bondage to decay and brought into the glorious freedom of the children of God." (Romans 8:20-21 NIV)

Sin holds people in bondage. That fact is clearly established throughout Paul's letters. Sin has also caused all creation to fall from the perfect state in which God created it. The world physically decays and experiences conflict so that it cannot fulfill its intended purpose. One day God will liberate and transform all creation. Until then, it waits in eager expectation for God's "time." Christ provided the means for this restoration. When the time arrives, all of creation (meaning every created thing and being) will be as God created it to be—perfect, eternal, and fulfilling its intended function to praise God. All of creation is summed up in Christ; all creation exists because of Christ; all creation will one day offer praise to Christ. The dirtiness of sin will be cleansed away, and true and lasting peace will be established (see Isaiah 11:1-10; Revelation 21:1-5).

This verse does not teach that God will eventually save everyone, although many would like to believe this. The doctrine of Universalism, as this belief is called, seems to make God a little easier to understand and a little less harsh on sinners. In the end, every knee will bow, but for some, it will be too late. Christ will bring those elected and saved, and all creation with them, to be united under him in this glorious kingdom. Those who have refused to believe (whether Jews or Gentiles) will face the consequences of their unbelief (Matthew 25:31-46).

HAPPY ENDING
If you read a good murder mystery or see a well-done suspense movie, chances are you don't know "whodunit" until the end. The author or screenwriter gives you clues all along, but you probably won't catch on until the final, climactic scene, when all the tensions are resolved and all the loose ends are tied up. That's what Paul portrays as God unfolds his plan for the world. We probably won't truly grasp God's plan until the "final scene," but he has certainly given us plenty of clues. And, unlike a suspense novel, in God's great drama of redemption, he revealed the main character early on: Jesus, the unique Son of God. When you feel as though your world is too confusing or completely out of control, remember: God is sovereign; he is in charge. God's purpose to save you cannot be thwarted, no matter what evil Satan may bring. God has it all worked out; the ending is already written. For the Christian, it's a happy one.

1:11 **In him we were also chosen, having been predestined according to the plan of him who works out everything in conformity with the purpose of his will.**[NIV] God began to reveal his great mystery at the death and resurrection of Christ. "In him," refers back to Christ ("in union with Christ"). Another part of that mystery made itself clear as the early church (made up mostly of converted Jews) understood that this plan was also available to Gentiles (see Acts 10:34-35).

Up until 1:11, Paul was speaking to Jews and Gentiles alike. In 2:11, Paul made a distinction between the backgrounds of the Jewish believers and Gentile believers. In verses 11-14, however, he identified the two separate groups with the pronouns he used.

The wording in these verses includes both the first person (we, our) and the second person (you). The word "we" refers specifically to Jewish believers (Paul being one of them). While it is true that believing Jews and Gentiles alike will receive God's blessings, the Jews were called first (Romans 1:16); they were *chosen*. Christ will be the Head of all things (1:10), including a body of believers made up of Jews ("we") and Gentiles ("you," 1:13).

In the Old Testament, the word "chosen" refers to the nation of Israel as God's portion or inheritance:

- "But as for you, the LORD took you and brought you . . . out of Egypt, to be the people of his inheritance, as you now are." (Deuteronomy 4:20 NIV)
- "But they are your people, your inheritance that you brought out by your great power and your outstretched arm." (Deuteronomy 9:29 NIV)
- "The LORD will inherit Judah as his portion in the holy land and will again choose Jerusalem." (Zechariah 2:12 NIV)

The Jews were *predestined according to [God's] plan* that would ultimately be accomplished in Jesus Christ (born into the nation of Israel) and finalized at the end of time. God chose the Jews to be the people through whom the rest of the world could find salvation. But this did not mean that the entire Jewish nation would be saved; only those who receive Jesus Christ as their Messiah and Savior will receive God's blessings (see Romans 9–11). When God offered salvation to the Gentiles, he did not exclude the Jews. God's kingdom will include all Jews and Gentiles who have accepted the offer of salvation. Both Jews and Gentiles will also make up the group that does not believe and so receives God's punishment. The inclusion of Jewish believers in salvation was the plan of God *who works out everything in conformity with the purpose of his will.* In the same way that God predestined Israel to be the elect nation, he predestined the spiritual Israelites, the believers in Christ, to be an eternal gift to himself. As a refrain carried through from 1:5 and 1:9, Paul repeated that everything is under God's sovereign control. The words reinforce the certainty of these events. Because God controls everything, he will carry out his plan according to his purpose and will, bringing it to completion in his time.

1:12 In order that we, who were the first to hope in Christ, might be for the praise of his glory.NIV The word "we" refers to Jewish believers—those who recognized their promised Messiah. The Jews *were the first to hope in Christ.* This could mean that ages before the arrival of Christ, the Jews had set their hope on their coming Messiah (see Acts 28:20), or it could mean that the Jews were the first to believe in Christ because the gospel was preached first to them (see, for example, John 1:11; 8:30; Acts 1:8; 3:26; 13:45-46).

Paul pointed out the timing of God's plan of bringing the gospel message through the Jews ("we . . . the first") and then offering it to the Gentiles. Yet throughout this eulogy, Paul continued to focus on the unity in Christ of all believers, resulting in *the praise of his glory.* This phrase, appearing in 1:6 and later in 1:14, reveals once again God's ultimate plan for all his creation— to glorify himself.

1:13 And you also were included in Christ when you heard the word of truth, the gospel of your salvation. Having believed, you were marked in him with a seal, the promised Holy Spirit.[NIV] Because the word "we" in 1:12 most likely refers to Jews, the words "you also" refer to Gentile believers who were *included in Christ* along with the Jewish believers. The believers, both Jews and Gentiles, *heard the word of truth* (see also Colossians 1:5; 2 Timothy 2:15; James 1:18), also called *the gospel of your salvation.* The gospel conveys the truth, which is able to sanctify the believer. But while hearing brings knowledge, it does

THE SEAL OF THE SPIRIT

The Spirit marks the beginning of the Christian experience.

- We cannot belong to Christ without his Spirit. . . .Romans 8:9
- We cannot be united to Christ without his Spirit. . .1 Corinthians 6:17
- We cannot be adopted as his children
  without his Spirit. . . . . .Romans 8:14-17;
                                                              Galatians 4:6-7
- We cannot be in the body of Christ
  except by baptism in the Spirit. . . . . .1 Corinthians 12:13

The Spirit is the power of our new lives.

- The Spirit lives within us. . . . . .1 Corinthians 6:19
- The Spirit changes us from within,
  helping us produce "fruit." . . . . .Galatians 5:22-23
- The Spirit helps us become more like Christ. . . . .2 Corinthians 3:18;
                                                              Ephesians 3:16-19

The Spirit unites the Christian community.

- The Spirit is building us into a holy dwelling. . . . .Ephesians 2:22
- The Spirit can be experienced by all
  and works through all. . . . . .1 Corinthians 12:4-11

not bring salvation. These people also *believed.* When they believed, they were then *marked in him* showing that they were *included in Christ.*

What exactly did Paul mean by the "seal," which he then identified as *the promised Holy Spirit?* In the ancient world, a seal was a form of identification used to authenticate and protect legal documents. A uniquely designed stone worn on a ring or necklace was used to mark clay or wax (Genesis 38:18; Esther 3:10; Isaiah 29:11) on a document. In religious usage, "seal" meant that the power of the deity protected the bearer and was available to him or her. The Jews tied the word in with the covenant of circumcision; that is, the person was "sealed" as a member of God's people through this act (Genesis 17:9-14; Romans 4:11). Heathen religions would "seal" their devotees with tattoos of the emblems of their cult.

The meaning of this seal of the Holy Spirit has received a variety of interpretations. Some point to a particular form of water baptism, others to a "baptism of the Holy Spirit" resulting in the manifestation of some spiritual gift (such as speaking in tongues). Most likely this seal of the Holy Spirit means that God marks his people as his own through the presence of the Holy Spirit in their lives. The Holy Spirit fills us with a sense of God's love (Romans 5:5), assures us that God has adopted us as his children (Romans 8:15-16), and helps us to manifest our Christlikeness. The sealing by the Spirit is a once-and-for-all act that gives us continued assurance that we are God's children, entitled to his riches and goodness, now as well as in eternity.

The "promised" Holy Spirit could refer to the fact that the Holy Spirit was promised in the Old Testament (Isaiah 32:15; 44:3; Joel 2:28;) and was promised by Jesus to his disciples (John 14:16-17, 25-26; 15:26; 16:7-15; Acts 1:4-5; 2:38-39). It could also mean that the Holy Spirit is the One through whom God fulfills his promises to believers (as is the thought in 1:14).

After Christ returned to heaven, he would be spiritually present everywhere through the Holy Spirit. The Holy Spirit came so that God would be within his followers after Christ returned to heaven. At Pentecost (Acts 2), the Holy Spirit came upon all who believed in Jesus. Believers received the Holy Spirit (were "sealed" by him) when they received Jesus Christ. As recorded in the book of Acts, the receiving of the Holy Spirit was the authenticating "seal" of salvation (see, for example, Acts 8:14-17; 10:44-48). The transformation that the Holy Spirit makes in a believer's life (as described in Galatians 5:22-23) undeniably marks God's presence in and ownership of that life.

**1:14 Who is a deposit guaranteeing our inheritance until the
redemption of those who are God's possession—to the praise
of his glory.**^{NIV} "Who" refers to the Holy Spirit. The word "deposit"
is also translated "guarantee," "pledge," or "earnest" (see Jeremiah
38:17-20). The word was used in ancient times to describe an
engagement ring or a down payment. The deposit was like earnest
money put down on a purchase—it was a partial payment promis-
ing that the buyer would complete the transaction and pay the
full amount. The deposit was binding. In the same way, God's
"deposit" of the Holy Spirit in believers' lives is the first payment
of all the treasures that will be theirs. And the deposit binds both
parties. We have the Spirit now but will experience him even more
fully when we live with Christ forever (Romans 8:23; 2 Corinthians 1:21-22; 5:5). God will keep all his promises *(guaranteeing our
inheritance)*; believers are to carry out God's mission on earth. The
presence of the Holy Spirit in us demonstrates the genuineness of
our faith, proves that we are God's children, and secures eternal life
for us. His power works in us to transform us now, and what we
experience now is a taste of the total change we will experience in
eternity.

SIGNED, SEALED, DELIVERED
In modern Greek, the word used for "guarantee" now means
"engagement ring." Most married couples clearly remember
when, where, and how they agreed to get married. It is usually
a very romantic and pleasant story. Unfortunately, half of all
couples who become engaged never make it down the aisle—
something happens, and someone breaks the engagement.
Ephesians 1:14 says that the Holy Spirit is a "deposit guaranteeing our inheritance" for those who belong to Christ. The
Spirit is, in effect, our "engagement ring" that shows that we
belong to Christ until our "wedding day"—the day we go to be
with him forever. And our great confidence is this: God, unlike
most people, never breaks his promises. You never need to
worry about your standing with him. If you have trusted in
Christ, you are his—signed, sealed, and delivered—forever.

The believers' inheritance is certain. God will not renege on
his pledge. Peter wrote, "In his great mercy he has given us new
birth into a living hope through the resurrection of Jesus Christ
from the dead, and into an inheritance that can never perish, spoil
or fade—kept in heaven for you" (1 Peter 1:3-4 NIV). Paul wrote
to the Corinthians, "[God] set his seal of ownership on us, and
put his Spirit in our hearts as a deposit, guaranteeing what is to
come" (2 Corinthians 1:22 NIV).

However, believers will not receive their full inheritance *until the redemption of those who are God's possession.* "Redemption," as explained in 1:7, refers to Christ setting sinners free from slavery to sin. Redemption has been partly completed because Christ has already died for sin. The word "redemption" focuses on the time when God will completely free believers from the presence of sin (the word is used the same way in Romans 8:23). This redemption will occur for "God's possession," those who are "sealed" by the Holy Spirit through their belief in and acceptance of Christ as Savior.

As a final ringing note echoing 1:6 (praising God) and 1:12 (praising Jesus Christ), Paul declared that the Holy Spirit's work will be *to the praise of God's glory.*

PAUL'S PRAYER FOR THE EPHESIAN BELIEVERS / 1:15-23

As verses 3-14 are one long sentence in the Greek, so are verses 15-23. As verses 3-14 are an extended eulogy, verses 15-23 are an extended thanksgiving. Verses 15-16 are the thanksgiving proper; verses 17-19 are an intercessory prayer; verses 20-23 are a confession of praise for God's power.

1:15-16 Therefore I also, after I heard of your faith in the Lord Jesus and your love for all the saints, do not cease to give thanks for you, making mention of you in my prayers.NKJV After describing the glorious blessings given to believers (1:3-14), thoughts of the great promises of God led Paul to give praise and to pray for the church—the people chosen to receive those blessings. "Therefore" is also translated "for this reason." Paul could write confidently to the Ephesian believers, knowing that they were partakers of the benefits of salvation and the Spirit graciously given by God.

The phrase "after I heard of your faith" could mean that Paul had heard a good report of the Ephesians' growth in the faith. It could also be a way of including the believers in the surrounding churches. Paul knew the Ephesian church well but not all the surrounding churches. Yet he may have heard a positive report of all the churches in the area, and thus he could thank God for their faith and remember them in his prayers.

The Ephesians' "faith" reported to Paul referred not to their saving faith (Paul already knew about that in Ephesus and most likely assumed it for the other churches). Rather, Paul had heard of their general faithfulness and trustworthiness—both of which were exercised *in the Lord Jesus.* This title for Christ reveals his lordship over all believers. Then Paul complimented them for their *love for all the saints.* Believers show their faithfulness to Christ through their love for other believers. (For similar greetings, see Colossians 1:4; 2 Thessalonians 1:3.)

Paul did *not cease* to give thanks for these believers. That Paul made *mention* of them in his prayers (or "remembered" them in his prayers) demonstrates personal attention; Paul prayed for the Ephesian believers by name—interceding, thanking, and praising. Paul was truly a prayer warrior—remembering the churches in his personal prayers: for example, the Romans (Romans 1:9), the Philippians (Philippians 1:3-4), the Colossians (Colossians 1:3-4), and the Thessalonians (1 Thessalonians 1:2-3).

PRAYER POWER
Many churches—and many Christians—act as though truth were the only emphasis that matters. Just give us good preaching and sound doctrine, and everything else will fall in line. Solid preaching and doctrine are important; in fact, they are essential. But so is prayer. A church or individual Christian who gets a steady input of truth but little or no prayer is like a beautiful sports car without oil in the engine. It may look and sound great for a while, but sooner or later it will break down. Prayer is the oil that keeps us running. When we pray for others, we ask the Holy Spirit to strengthen them. That's why it's so important that we pray for one another as Ephesians 1:15-16 teaches. Prayer also unleashes his power in us—power to guide, convict, encourage, heal. If the church depended on your prayers, how long and how well would the church keep running? When you say to someone, "I'll keep you in prayer," be sure you do it.

1:17 I keep asking that the God of our Lord Jesus Christ, the glorious Father, may give you the Spirit of wisdom and revelation, so that you may know him better.^NIV Paul prayed to the only One truly capable of hearing and answering. Paul described him in two ways: (1) *the God of our Lord Jesus Christ*—most likely repeating and abbreviating 1:3 above, where Paul introduced his letter praising "the God and Father of our Lord Jesus Christ," and (2) *the glorious Father*—the only One to whom all glory belongs.

Paul kept asking on behalf of these believers that God would give them *the Spirit of wisdom and revelation.* Paul was referring to the Holy Spirit. Some have taken this to mean the human spirit, but this section talks about thanksgiving for what God has done. Thus, Paul most likely was referring to the Holy Spirit. It is also true that only by the Holy Spirit can believers obtain these gifts.

The Holy Spirit gives "wisdom" (see also 1:8)—the ability to see life from God's perspective, to have discernment. He also gives "revelation," which refers to enlightened understanding, insight into God himself and the mysteries of divine truth. (See 1 Corinthians 2:14, 16 and Colossians 1:9.)

GETTING TO KNOW YOU
Paul prayed for the believers to know God better. How do you get to know someone? By reading biographical information or historical data about him or her? That will help you know a lot *about* that person, but it won't enable you to actually *know* him. If you want to get to know someone, you have to spend time with that person. There is no shortcut, no microwave process. The same holds true with God. Reading the Bible and great works of theology and devotional material is wonderful, but there is no substitute for knowing God personally. What about you? Do you really *know* God, or do you just know *about* him? The difference is in spending time with him. Study Jesus' life in the Gospels to see what he was like on earth two thousand years ago, and get to know him in prayer now. Personal knowledge of Christ will change your life.

1:18-19 I pray also that the eyes of your heart may be enlightened in order that you may know the hope to which he has called you.[NIV] For the Jew, the heart was the core of personality, the total inner person, the center of thought and moral judgment. The imagery of the *eyes of your heart* pictures an ability to see the reality of our hope. Tying verses 17 and 18 together, Paul prayed that the believers would receive wisdom and revelation so that their inner self would be constantly *enlightened* (the Greek verb is in the perfect tense, referring to a past action with continuous results). Some have identified baptism as the time of this enlightenment. See Colossians 1:12-13, which may be baptism liturgy. Most likely, Paul refers to the illumination of conversion

> If ever man is to come to a knowledge of God . . . two veils must be taken away: that which hides God's mind and that which clouds our heart. God in his mercy removes both. Thus our knowledge of God, first to last, is his gracious gift.
> *J. I. Packer*

(see 2 Corinthians 4:4, 6). Just as God's first act in the physical world was to create light where there had been only darkness (Genesis 1:1-5), so he gives light to the re-created individual (John 1:4, 9) by means of the Spirit's wisdom and revelation. With this enlightenment, they would *know* the truth of three realities:

1. "the hope to which he has called you" (1:18)

2. "the riches of his glorious inheritance in the saints" (1:18)
3. "his incomparably great power" (1:19)

First, Paul prayed that believers would be enlightened with the truth about their future (*the hope to which he has called you* NIV). Believers look forward to a future inheritance (Colossians 1:5) as well as blessings in this present world (1:19; Colossians 1:27) because of an action by God in the past (election). Believers' hope is not a vague feeling that the future will be positive, but it is complete assurance that God will do all that he has promised. This complete certainty comes through the Holy Spirit (1:14). We expect it to happen, trust God to bring it about, and patiently await its arrival. (For more on hope, see Romans 8:23-24; Ephesians 4:4; 1 Thessalonians 1:3; 1 Peter 3:15.)

The riches of his glorious inheritance in the saints.NIV Second, Paul prayed that the believers would be enlightened with the truth about the *riches of his glorious inheritance.* This is the second of six times that Paul used his characteristic word "riches" in this letter—here it pictures the value of this inheritance (see also 1:7). This phrase means that, in the last days, God will inherit his people, his precious possession, by bringing them to be with him forever.

And his incomparably great power for us who believe. That power is like the working of his mighty strength.NIV Third, Paul prayed that the believers would be enlightened with the truth about God's *incomparably great power for us who believe.* Each of these three truths builds on the previous one: The present basis for the riches and hope (the reason believers can hold on to the truth and certainty of God's promises) is the fact that the promises are rooted in God's great power. In this phrase, Paul used four nearly synonymous Greek words to express God's comprehensive power. Each word, by itself, has a slightly different focus: (1) "power" *(dunamis)* means capability or potential; (2) "working" *(energeian)* means effective or active power; (3) "mighty" (or "might," *kratous*) means a force that overcomes resistance (this word is used only of God, never of believers); and (4) "strength" *(ischuos)* refers to bodily or muscular strength in humans; inherent, vital power in God. Taken together, the four words exhibit God's all-inclusive power.

> The same power that brought Christ back from the dead is operative within those who are Christ's. The Resurrection is an ongoing thing.
> *Leon Morris*

The variety in these words underscores the completeness of God's power. Because of his power, believers know that:

- God is on their side, ready to help them meet each and every obstacle;
- God's power is never stagnant or out of commission—it is always actively working on their behalf;
- God is always fighting against the forces of evil on believers' behalf;
- no human strength or spiritual power from the evil world (not even Satan himself) can deter or change God's inherent power.

Only God's power can change weak human beings into strong believers who are willing to sacrifice everything for the God who loves them.

1:20 Which he exerted in Christ when he raised him from the dead and seated him at his right hand in the heavenly realms.NIV After impressively describing the completeness of God's power, Paul pointed out three instances when God's power was *exerted* (using the Greek word *energesen,* the same root word for the "working" of God's power in 1:19): (1) raising Christ from the dead (2) exalting Christ to his present position of authority (3) appointing him to be head over the church:

1. The resurrection of Christ from the dead was a clear working of God's power—only God can bring life from death. Christ's resurrection assures us that God will also raise our bodies (Romans 6:8-11; 8:11). The same power that raised Christ after his death is available to believers. It is transmitted through the Head (Christ) to the body (the church, the believers).
2. The exaltation of Christ to highest authority with God was also a clear working of God's power. Christ had humbled himself to live as a human and accomplish our redemption and then was returned by God to the highest position with him (John 3:31; Ephesians 4:10; Philippians 2:6-11). Christ is *seated* in a place of honor, at God's *right hand* (see Matthew 26:64; Acts 2:34ff; 7:55; Romans 8:34; Colossians 3:1; Hebrews 1:3, 13; 8:1; 10:12; 12:2; 1 Peter 3:22). According to ancient practice, the seat at the right hand signified a position of equality. Christ will remain there until all his enemies have been overcome (1 Corinthians 15:25). His remaining seated symbolizes his finished work and supreme authority.

    The reference to *the heavenly realms* refers to God's presence. Christ entered heaven with a physical body (Acts 1:9). This is probably an allusion to Psalm 110:1, a verse frequently quoted in the New Testament as key proof of the exaltation of Christ. The prophecies of the king of Israel find their highest fulfillment when applied to the person of Christ.

God used his power not to blast people or do amazing tricks
(as the gods of mythology were said to do). Instead, God's
power raised Christ from the dead, defeating Satan and promis-
ing resurrection to all believers. His power exalted Christ to a
position of authority where he intercedes with God on behalf
of believers (Romans 8:34; Hebrews 7:25) and from where he
will exercise leadership over all creation.

3. Having been raised from the dead, Christ is now the head
   of the church, the ultimate authority over the world. Jesus
   is the Messiah, God's Anointed One, the One Israel longed
   for, the One who would fix their broken world. As Christians
   we can be confident that God has won the final victory and
   is in control of everything. We need not fear any dictator or
   nation, death, or Satan himself. The contract has been signed
   and sealed; we are waiting just a short while for delivery.
   Romans 8:38-39 states that nothing can separate us from
   God and his love.

UNDISPUTED CHAMPION
How would you feel about climbing into the ring with a world-
class heavyweight boxing contender? Do the words "fear and
trembling" come to mind? But suppose you could enter the ring
with the undisputed heavyweight champion standing in your
corner. Now the fear and trembling belong to your opponent.
Death is the enemy no one could conquer, the one that held
us powerless in its cold, cruel grip. That is, *until* Jesus came
and conquered death, breaking its bondage over us forever.
Because of this, we can live freely, without fear. We can risk;
we can attempt great things for God, knowing no failure is fatal
with him in our corner. He has conquered death; he reigns over
all. We can live as his victorious, liberated people. Do you draw
your strength from Christ? Stay committed to him and unified
with him.

**1:21 Far above all rule and authority, power and dominion,
and every title that can be given, not only in the present age
but also in the one to come.**[NIV] Christ's ultimate authority, his
lordship, will be *far above* any other. The "above" indicates
superiority. Paul explained that all the rulers, authorities,
powers, and dominions in heaven and on earth, of both the
visible and invisible world (physical government and spiritual
forces), come under the authority of Christ himself. Paul listed
titles and names, adding even a generic phrase *(and every title
that can be given)* to clarify that whatever power exists *not only
in the present age but also in the one to come* will be under

Christ's authority. Some have seen in these words hierarchies
of angel princes. Others have seen parallels to the spiritual
enemies of Christians—law, sin, the flesh, and death. Paul
listed these because of people's belief that the world was inhab-
ited by powers and beings that worked against humanity. Christ
has no equal and no rival. He is supreme over all other beings.
These words ought to encourage believers, because the higher
the honor of Christ, the Head, the higher the honor of his
people.

ENTROPY
Entropy is the law of the universe. The sun will burn out,
the rain forest is vanishing, species become extinct by the
thousands every year, and your car falls apart by the mile.
Everything wears out, falls down, disintegrates. Many people
think that if there is nothing more to life than what we can see,
touch, taste, and experience, the best we can do is try to enjoy
the ride while it lasts because there's a nasty crash at the end.
But Ephesians 1:21 teaches that there is hope. Instead of the
world just fizzling out, we are heading toward a definite conclusion where Christ is Lord and God will make all things right.
Christians are called to proclaim truth to a world that embraces
falsehood, light to a world that dwells in darkness, and hope to
a world that has given in to despair. Entropy is the law of the
universe, but Christ is Lord over the universe. Rely on his
all-sufficient power for your daily needs.

**1:22 And God placed all things under his feet and appointed him
to be head over everything for the church.**NIV Paul probably
had a psalm in mind as he wrote these words. This alludes to
Psalm 8:6, a kingly messianic psalm describing sovereign power
and enthronement. Christ is the obvious application for the verse.
Just as the psalm writer described people as having dominion on
earth, so Paul described Christ as having dominion over all of
creation—*all things* will be placed *under his feet* (1 Corinthians
15:20-28).

Christ's headship is exercised in the present world through
his leadership over *the church.* God appointed Christ to be the
head over everything for the church. This can be taken two
ways: (1) Christ is over all things for the sake of the church
(that is, the church receives the benefit of his universal headship); (2) Christ is the head of the church and in this position
controls everything in all of creation.

**1:23 And the church is his body; it is filled by Christ, who fills
everything everywhere with his presence.**NLT That Christ is

the leader, or head, implies unity with the *church,* Christ's
body. Paul used the analogy elsewhere when he wrote about the
interrelationships of believers in the church (Romans 12:4-5;
1 Corinthians 12:22-27; Colossians 1:18-19). This passage
focuses on Christ as the head of that body, the church (see
also 4:4, 12, 16; 5:30). The church is not a building (or all the
church buildings on earth)—it includes all believers in a living,
growing, moving, working organism deriving existence and
power from Christ. The church obeys Christ's commands to
carry out his work in the world.

All believers, as part of Christ's body, are *filled by Christ
who fills everything everywhere with his presence.* That Christ
"fills everything" could be interpreted several ways: (1) The
church contains the fullness of Christ—he fills it with himself;
(2) the church contains gifts and blessings that only Christ can
give; (3) the church fills up Christ—as the church grows, it
completes Christ.

HEALTHY BODY
Try an experiment. Get your Bible study or prayer group to
finish this sentence: *The church is* _____. You will
undoubtedly get many different answers. But Ephesians 1:23
tells us that the church is *Christ's body,* filled with him. Just as
Jesus is God in a form that we can grasp, that we can understand, the church is to present Jesus to the world in a form it
can understand. We are his hands, feet, muscles, tendons,
voice. If Christ is truly the Head of the church, what does that
say about the role of the pastor(s), elders, deacons, worship
leaders, and other members? If we are truly his body, what
does that say about the role we are to play at our jobs, in our
schools, in our relationships?

While (3) probably gives the truer meaning for the Greek
word (*pleroma,* "that which fills," rather than "that which is
filled"), nowhere does the New Testament say that Christ is somehow incomplete without the church. Therefore, a combination of
(1) and (2) would seem more correct—Christ fills all things with
himself and with his blessings, bringing all believers to the state
of obedience and praise for which God created them (as in 1:10;
4:10, 13, 16). The church is being filled with and by Christ, who
fills all things totally. Thus, Christ, who is the fullness of God
(Colossians 1:19), finds full expression in the church.

By Christ's resurrection and exaltation, he is head over all things
for the church. Christ fills the church and then uses the gifts he
bestows to fulfill his mission—revealing himself to the world and

drawing people to himself by that witness. When reading Ephesians, it is important to remember that this epistle was written primarily to the entire church, not to an individual or even to one
congregation. Christ is the Head, and we are the body of his
church. The image of the body shows the church's unity. Each
member is involved with all the others as they go about doing
Christ's work on earth. We should not attempt to work, serve, or
worship on our own. We need the entire body.

Ephesians 2

The style of using lengthy sentences continues from chapter 1 into this chapter, in which verses 1-7 are one sentence in the Greek. To help understand the first seven verses, note that the subject of that Greek sentence is "God" (2:4) and that there are three main verbs: (1) "made . . . alive with" (2:5), (2) "raised . . . up with" (2:6), and (3) "seated . . . with" (2:6). The object of each of these verbs is "us," referring to believers. God has made us alive, raised us up, and seated us with Christ.

2:1 As for you, you were dead in your transgressions and sins.[NIV] This verse is a continuation of 1:19-23, which speaks of the resurrection power imparted to Christ's body. The phrase "as for you" identifies those who were *dead in . . . trangressions and sins* before they met Christ. This refers not only to eventual physical death or to the sinners' ultimate eternal state; it also refers to a very real "death" in this life. People who are spiritually dead have no communication with God. These people are physically alive, but their sins have rendered them spiritually unresponsive, alienated from God, and thus incapable of experiencing the full life that God could give them. (See also Ezekiel 37:1-14; Romans 6:23; 7:10, 24; Colossians 2:13.)

Unbelievers are dead "in" their *transgressions and sins.* The sins and transgressions do not cause the death; instead, sinners and their sins are together in the same sphere of death. The significance of the two words "transgressions" and "sins" may be no more than repetition for emphasis (a common Hebrew writing technique—see also 1:7). The root meaning of "transgressions" suggests a fall or lapse, while the root meaning of "sins" implies an innate state of corruption. Both words reveal people's inability to please God and live as they should. The plural of both words further emphasizes the natural tendency of humans to continue in sin. Unbelievers' constant sin and rebellion against God portray their spiritual death.

YOU WERE DEAD
If someone handed you a couple of pills and said, "Swallow these," would you do it? Not likely. However, if you were in a medical office and the person speaking was a doctor who had just told you that you would die unless you took the pills, you would be more likely to do so. Sometimes you have to know how bad the bad news is before you can appreciate the good news. Paul tells us how bad the bad news is: "As for you, you were dead in your transgressions and sins." *Dead.* Not sick, not dying, not having an off day—*dead.* What can dead people do to help themselves? Not much . . . in fact, absolutely nothing. That is why God, in his mercy, had to reach out to us in his unfathomable love: a love that would sacrifice his only Son for us. God has given you your diagnosis. Have you understood it? He has also given you the remedy. Have you taken it?

2:2 You used to live just like the rest of the world, full of sin, obeying Satan, the mighty prince of the power of the air. He is the spirit at work in the hearts of those who refuse to obey God.NLT "Transgressions" and "sins" (2:1) reveal spiritual death, but they are acted out by people who are physically alive. Before the Ephesian believers came to Christ, they *used to live* in their transgressions and sins. The word "live" could also be translated "walk," describing the conduct or direction of one's life. Instead of moving toward God, those who have not accepted Christ can only move in one direction—away from God, walking in their sins. They could not and did not follow God. Paul described three marks of unbelievers:

1. They lived *like the rest of the world.* This refers to the world's accepted, but immoral, lifestyles and godless motives. Jesus warned his followers: "If the world hates you, keep in mind that it hated me first. If you belonged to the world, it would love you as its own. As it is, you do not belong to the world, but I have chosen you out of the world. That is why the world hates you" (John 15:18-19 NIV). People who live like the rest of the world cannot also follow Jesus (Romans 12:2; Galatians 1:4).
2. They followed *the mighty prince of the power of the air.* This prince is Satan. The passage focuses on Satan's reality as an evil power with a certain amount of control in the world. The Bible pictures Satan as ruling an evil spiritual kingdom—the demons and those who are against Christ. "Satan" means "the accuser." Paul calls Satan the "devil" in 4:27 and 6:11. In 6:16, he calls him the "evil one." How is Satan "the mighty prince of the power of the air," as Paul called him here? The Greek word *archon* means "ruler" and refers to Satan's control.

In the Old Testament, angels and spirit powers operated in heaven (Job 1:6). The "air" *(tou aeros)* refers to the space around the earth, and thus, this is Satan's sphere of influence. Though Satan's influence is great among unbelievers, his power is limited because he is a defeated enemy. He cannot separate believers from the love of God.

Satan is also called *the spirit at work in the hearts of those who refuse to obey God.* That Satan and his demons work in unbelievers makes his evil kingdom very real. Paul wanted the Ephesians to recognize Satan's work as a present threat. The evil powers at work rival the work of the Holy Spirit (1:21). People who have not surrendered to God or decided to obey are energized by the power of evil. The force of the evil spirit is seen in those who actively disobey God both in faith and action (2 Thessalonians 1:8). These people live in constant rebellion and opposition to God.

3. They were enslaved to "gratifying the cravings of [the] sinful nature" (2:3). This is the third mark of unbelievers, described in the following verse.

2:3 All of us also lived among them at one time, gratifying the cravings of our sinful nature and following its desires and thoughts.^{NIV} *All of us* (Jews and Gentiles alike) were at one time separated from God because of our disobedience. Romans 3:23 states, "All have sinned and fall short of the glory of God" (NKJV; see also Romans 2:1-9; 3:9).

Throughout the ages, human beings have lived in sin and disobedience, and Paul's audience (now believers) *lived among them,* that is, among those people. Though believers, the Ephesians still lived among the sinful unbelievers, but they no longer participated in the sinful lifestyles. Unbelievers cannot follow

> Our old nature is no more extinct than the devil, but God's will is that the dominion of both should be broken.
> *John R. W. Stott*

God because they do not know him; instead, they live enslaved to *the cravings of [the] sinful nature, . . . following its desires.* The philosophy "if it feels good do it" is not unique to the twentieth century. "Gratifying" means that they did whatever felt natural to them. The "sinful nature" refers to people's natural state without God. That nature is self-centered, enslaved to its own desires.

The fact that all people, without exception, commit sin proves that everyone has a sinful nature. We are lost in sin and cannot save ourselves. Does this mean that only Christians do good? Of course not. Many people do good to others; on a relative scale, many are moral, kind, and law-abiding. Comparing these people to criminals, we would say that they are very good indeed. But on God's absolute scale, *no one* is good enough to earn salvation ("you were dead in your transgressions and sins," 2:1). While it is true that unbelievers do good works, they are still separated from God. Sin corrupts everything—our actions, thoughts, desires, will, intellect, and reasoning. Only through being united with Christ's perfect life can we become good in God's sight.

"Sinful nature" is the Greek word *sarx*. It also has been translated as "flesh." When we become believers, our sinful nature still exists. But when we submit our lives to the Holy Spirit, he transforms us and our sinful natures. This is a supernatural process. We must never underestimate the power of our sinful nature, and we must never attempt to subdue it in our own strength. God provides for victory over sin—he sends the Holy Spirit to live in us and give us power. But our ability to restrain the desires of the sinful nature depends on how much we're willing to depend on God and his mercy (2:4-5).

Like the rest, we were by nature objects of wrath.^{NIV} The phrase "objects of wrath" is a Jewish idiom for those who deserve God's punishment. The fact that this is *by nature* reveals that this is humanity's natural state apart from God's redeeming grace. But the word "wrath" contains a seed of hope. Those who were once "objects of wrath" can accept Christ and experience redemption and salvation. That occurs "by grace" (see 2:5). However, those who persist in their rebellion against God, whether Jews or Gentiles, will experience the wrath of God (John 3:36; Romans 1:18–2:29).

ADDICTED
Those addicted to drugs report that the first encounter with heroin or crack or alcohol is a thrill, a rush. But afterward, it ceases to be fun. From then on, the addict is just killing the pain. Sin is like that. The first time, it—whatever "it" is (lust, greed, lying)—is a thrill. After that, it becomes a tyrant, a heartless slave driver. You don't use it; it uses you. In which areas of your life are you still in bondage to sin and the author of sin? Confess them to God, acknowledging your inability to control them. Thank him for the provision he made through the cross of Christ. Take those sins that have enslaved you and owned you and leave them there. Allow God to set you free from their tyranny by the power of his love, his light, his grace.

2:4 But God, who is rich in mercy, because of His great love with which He loved us.^{NKJV} The subject of Paul's lengthy sentence throughout verses 1-7 is God. The first three verses of this chapter present a hopeless humanity—trapped in sin, under Satan's power, unable to save itself. Then follow the small but glorious words "but God." Behind those two words lies a cosmic plan so huge in scope and so vast in love that the human mind cannot fully comprehend it—all we can do is humbly receive it. Instead of leaving sinful humanity to live worthless and hopeless lives ending only in death, God acted. *How* God acted is explained in the verses that follow. *Why* he acted is explained in this verse and in 2:7.

God acted on behalf of humanity because he *is rich in mercy.* As God is rich in grace (1:7), so he is rich in mercy (see the chart on page 18, "God's Riches Given to Us." The word "rich" indicates the bountiful nature of God's mercy—beyond our comprehension, an inexhaustible storehouse. What is "mercy"? The word has its roots in the Hebrew word *hesed.* Mercy was seen as a basic attribute of God, sometimes called "lovingkindness" or "compassion." This word describes the outworking of God's love toward people and is shown in his lovingkindness toward them even though they do not deserve it (Psalm 51:1; Jeremiah 9:24; Hosea 2:19; Jonah 4:2).

BUT GOD
We were dead in our sins, *but God* . . . We were rebels against him, *but God* . . . We were enslaved by Satan and our sinful natures, *but God* . . . These may be the two most welcome words in all of Scripture: "but God." God could have left us spiritually dead, in rebellion against him and in bondage to our sins. *But he didn't.* He did not save us because of, but rather in spite of, what he saw in us. In addition to thanking him for what he has done for us, we should also show humble patience and tolerance for others who seem unworthy or undeserving of our love and compassion. They may be spiritually dull, rebellious, and even antagonistic toward God. So were we; *but God loved us anyway.* Can we do less for fellow sinners?

God also acted on behalf of humanity *because of His great love.* The Greek word for love, *agape,* is used. It means the self-less love that seeks the best for others. While God could have simply destroyed all people because of their sin, he chose instead to show mercy and love. The prophet Zephaniah wrote, "The LORD has taken away your punishment, he has turned back your enemy. The LORD, the King of Israel, is with you; never again will you fear any harm" (Zephaniah 3:15 NIV). Sinful people cannot even approach the holy God, but God extended his love to them, knowing that only he could give salvation to them. Such love is "great" and beyond human understanding.

This love was directed toward *us,* meaning Jews and Gentiles alike. God's riches of grace, mercy, and love were meant for all kinds of people from the beginning—Jews and Gentiles—and all people are offered salvation and life in Christ.

2:5 Made us alive with Christ even when we were dead in transgressions.[NIV] This verse finishes the thought begun in 2:1, we *were dead;* now we are *made alive.* Verses 5 and 6 describe three acts accomplished by God. Each believer has been (1) made alive with Christ, (2) raised up with Christ, and (3) seated with Christ. Each of these three phrases begins with the same prefix in the Greek, *sun,* on the verb. The prefix means "together with," indicating that each believer will share these experiences with all other believers and with Christ himself.

Verse 4 explains why God acted on our behalf. But *how* did God act? In contrast to the spiritual and eternal death that was the fate of sinful humanity (2:1-3), God *made us alive.* "Made alive" means that we are "saved" (this phrase is repeated in 2:8 and elaborated on there). When Christ rose from the dead, so did all the members of his body by virtue of God's uniting them with Christ.

Unbelievers were dead in sins, but they appropriated the new life with Christ when they received salvation. "Made alive" is often used as a synonym for "raised from the dead" (see John 5:21; 6:63; Romans 4:17; 1 Corinthians 15:12-23). The only way spiritually dead people can have a relationship with God is to be made alive. And God is the only person who can accomplish that, which he did through his Son, Jesus Christ. Christ defeated sin and death through his death and resurrection, thus offering spiritual life to those dead in sins. Paul explained this in other letters, for it is a key doctrine of the Christian faith:

- *Now if we died with Christ, we believe that we will also live with him. For we know that since Christ was raised from the dead, he cannot die again; death no longer has mastery over him. The death he died, he died to sin once for all; but the life he lives, he lives to God. In the same way, count yourselves dead to sin but alive to God in Christ Jesus. (Romans 6:8-11 NIV)*

- *But if Christ is in you, though the body is dead because of sin, the Spirit is life because of righteousness. If the Spirit of him who raised Jesus from the dead dwells in you, he who raised Christ from the dead will give life to your mortal bodies also through his Spirit that dwells in you. (Romans 8:10-11 NRSV)*

■ *I have been crucified with Christ; it is no longer I who live, but Christ lives in me; and the life which I now live in the flesh I live by faith in the Son of God, who loved me and gave Himself for me. (Galatians 2:20 NKJV)*

■ *[You] having been buried with him in baptism and raised with him through your faith in the power of God, who raised him from the dead. When you were dead in your sins and in the uncircumcision of your sinful nature, God made you alive with Christ. He forgave us all our sins. (Colossians 2:12-13 NIV)*

Paul repeated the phrase "dead in transgressions" from 2:1 to contrast death with the gift of life. As "death" in 2:1 was living death as well as spiritual and eternal death, so "life" from God begins true life now both physically and spiritually and extends to eternity. This life is *with Christ* because he redeemed us, gave us this life, and was the first to be resurrected (Romans 8:11, 17). God did not require us to be good enough before he reached down to save us; he made us alive *when* we were dead. Thus, the only basis for salvation is God's grace.

Paul emphasized that we do not need to live any longer under sin's power. The penalty of sin and its power over us were miraculously destroyed by Christ on the cross. Through faith in Christ we stand acquitted, or not guilty, before God (Romans 3:21-22). God does not take us out of the world or make us robots—we will still feel like sinning, and sometimes we will sin. The difference is that before we became Christians, we were dead in sin and were slaves to our sinful nature. But now we are alive with Christ (see also Galatians 2:20).

By grace you have been saved. The verb form "have been saved" refers to a past event (accomplished by Christ) with present and ongoing results. Believers have already passed from death to life. Salvation is not something to be waited for but something that has already been delivered.

2:6 And God raised us up with Christ and seated us with him in the heavenly realms in Christ Jesus.[NIV] In addition to being "made alive" (2:5), believers are also *raised . . . up with Christ.* Christ was raised from death and left the tomb—an act accomplished by God's power alone, as Paul explained in 1:20. Believers have also been "raised." In addition to assurance of physical resurrection and glorification at the end of the age, believers participate in a new "resurrection" life from the moment they believe (see Colossians 2:12).

We conduct this new life in obedience to God, and thus it is

totally different from the life the world offers. As Christ was
raised from physical death, believers too are raised from spiritual
death to an entirely new kind of life. Believers will experience
physical death, but we are assured of resurrection from that death
and eternal life with God.

Finally, believers are *seated . . . with
him in the heavenly realms.* Christ has
taken his seat at the right hand of the
Father, indicating his finished work and
his victory over sin. Christ has been
exalted by God's great power (1:20).

> Christ rose again, but our
> sins did not; they are
> buried forever in his
> grave.   *John Brown*

Christians have tended to see this seating with Christ as a future
event, based on Jesus' words in Matthew 19:28 and Luke 22:30
as well as other verses that point to our future reign with Christ
(such as 2 Timothy 2:12; Revelation 20:4; 22:5). Yet Ephesians
teaches that we are seated with Christ *now.* We share with Christ
in his victory *now.* This view of our present status should help us
face our work and trials with greater hope! Believers, as heirs of
the kingdom along with Christ, are spiritually exalted from the
moment of salvation. We have a new citizenship—in heaven, no
longer just on earth: "For our citizenship is in heaven, from
which we also eagerly wait for the Savior, the Lord Jesus Christ"
(Philippians 3:20 NKJV). The power that raised and exalted Christ
also raised and exalted his people. That same power works daily
in believers, helping us live and work for God during our time in
the world.

Being made alive, being raised, and being seated in heaven occurs
in Christ Jesus. Christ Jesus was the forerunner—without his sacrifice for our sins, his resurrection, and his exaltation, humanity would
still be without hope. Because of Christ's resurrection, we know that
our bodies will also be raised from the dead (1 Corinthians 15:12-23).
Our eternal life with Christ is certain because we are united in his
powerful victory. We have been given the power to live as Christians
now (1:19), not in conformity to the world and its standards, but in
obedience to God (Romans 12:2). This metaphor pictures God sharing his glory and victory with his people, giving them the privilege
and authority of shared kingship. Believers can claim their royal
status *now,* for they are children of the King!

**2:7 That in the ages to come He might show the exceeding riches
of His grace in His kindness toward us in Christ Jesus.**NKJV
Here is the final and definitive reason for God's action on behalf
of humanity, his reason for making us alive, raising us, and seating us along with his Son in the heavenly realms. God wants
quite simply to *show the exceeding riches of his grace in his kind-*

ness toward us. The Greek word for "show" (or "show forth")
comes from legal terminology. God closes the case by presenting
the astounding evidence of his church, his people. The church
could only exist by God's love; the fact of its existence, the fact
that people have been offered salvation, reveals the abundance
of God's grace and kindness (see also 1:7; 2:4). Again, this was
accomplished only *in Christ Jesus.* Without Christ's sacrifice,
there would be no hope for a relationship with God. "For God so
loved the world that He gave His only begotten Son, that whoever believes in Him should not perish but have everlasting life"
(John 3:16 NKJV). The result? Eternal praise from those whom he
has saved (see 1:6, 12, 14).

To whom does God "show" this? Obviously the believers are
experiencing God's grace and kindness. But the believers, the
church, show God's grace and kindness to an unbelieving world.
The phrase "in the ages to come" refers to future ages on earth.
Throughout history, God will continually demonstrate his work.
As time goes by, his grace will be fully shown.

WHO ELSE BUT GOD?
There is an expression: "When you see a turtle on a fence post,
you know he didn't get there by himself." It's obvious that someone had to put the turtle up there. In a very real sense, Christians are turtles sitting atop fence posts, put there by the grace
of God. It's as if someone asked God, "How can I be sure you're
as loving and gracious as you say you are?" His response is
simply to display the church—flawed, sinful, capable of
stupidity and faithlessness—as Exhibit A, demonstrating his
infinite patience and mercy. How else would a group of such
obviously fallen men and women get together and do anything
for the glory of God? Who else but God would use people like
us? You are a display case for the grace of God. Demonstrate
his great kindness to you by sharing it with others. Use his
patience with you to witness to others.

2:8 For by grace you have been saved through faith.^{NKJV} Elaborat-
ing on the statement in 2:5, this verse repeats that it is *by grace*
that anyone is *saved.* Salvation includes being made alive, raised,
and seated with Christ as described in 2:5-6, and that occurs only
because of God's kindness toward undeserving people. "Grace"
refers to the multifaceted gift that God makes available to us
despite our unworthiness. Not only does God mercifully withhold
the judgment and punishment that we so clearly deserve, he
grants instead the almost unbelievable gifts of forgiveness, salvation, and eternal life. God's grace requires faith because the

moral and legal case against us leads to an inevitable verdict—
guilty. "Grace" means the forgiveness of our sins. It cannot be
earned by works or by any goodness in us. It is free and undeserved favor on us by Christ's faithful act of redemption.

Our salvation comes from God's
grace alone. "Through faith" could
refer to: (1) God's faithfulness to his
promises, (2) Christ's faithfulness in
his obedience to God by dying on the
cross, or (3) people's faith in accepting
salvation. In light of Paul's references
to the Ephesians' faith in 1:1 and 15,
he most likely meant "faith" to refer to

> The only thing that a
> man can contribute to
> his redemption is the sin
> from which he needs to
> be redeemed.
>
> *William Temple*

people's faith (#3 above). The way people obtain salvation is
through faith—simple acceptance of God's gift of salvation (see
also Romans 3:22, 25; Galatians 2:16).

And that not of yourselves; it is the gift of God.NKJV Lest
anyone should think that "faith" is a necessary work that
people must perform in order to receive salvation, Paul added
this phrase. It is unclear whether *that* refers back to "saved,"
"faith," or to the previous section. It is most likely that Paul is
referring back to his entire explanation of salvation in 2:4-8,
thus including "saved" and "faith" in his one word "that."
Thus, "faith" is also a gift. In any case, Paul is firm that absolutely nothing is of our own doing *(not of yourselves)*—not
salvation, not grace, not even the faith exercised to receive
salvation—everything *is the gift of God.* Salvation does not
come from our self-reliance or individualism but from God's
initiative. It is a gift to be thankfully accepted (see Romans
3:24-28; 1 Corinthians 1:29-31; Galatians 2:16).

2:9 **Not of works, lest anyone should boast.**NKJV Salvation is "not
of yourselves" (2:8), and it is *not of works.* In other words,
people can do nothing to earn salvation, and a person's faith itself
also is not to be considered a "work" or grounds that *anyone
should boast.*

People find it difficult to accept something so free, so willingly given, so available to anyone. We want to feel as though
we *did* something, that we somehow earned our salvation by our
merit. That was how the Judaizers (false teachers who said Christians had to obey all the Jewish laws) regarded their laws and
why they tried to impose them on the Gentiles—there had to be
a certain amount of law keeping and goodness on people's part
in order for them to receive salvation. But Paul's words are

unmistakable—if salvation is by God's grace and is accepted through faith, then it is "not of works." If salvation could be earned by good works, then people would, by nature, "boast" about their good works, compare the good-

> If there is to be in our celestial garment but one stitch of our own making we are all of us lost.
> *C. H. Spurgeon*

ness of their works to others' good works, and do good only to boast about it. Then, what would be "good enough" for salvation? But no one could ever be good enough to please a holy God. He casts aside all human effort and pride by offering salvation for free to all people by simple acceptance. People are given salvation on the grounds of God's grace alone.

NOT OF WORKS BUT OF GRACE

Acts 15:11	"On the contrary, we believe that we will be saved through the *grace* of the Lord Jesus, just as they will" (NRSV).
Acts 18:27	"On arriving, [Apollos] was a great help to those who by *grace* had believed" (NIV).
Romans 3:24	"Justified freely by His *grace* through the redemption that is in Christ Jesus" (NKJV).
Romans 4:16	"Therefore, the promise comes by faith, so that it may be by *grace* and may be guaranteed to all Abraham's offspring . . . to those who are of the faith of Abraham. He is the father of us all" (NIV).
Romans 11:6	"But if it is by *grace,* it is no longer on the basis of works, otherwise *grace* would no longer be *grace*" (NRSV).
Galatians 3:18	"For if the inheritance depends on the law, then it no longer depends on a promise; but God in his *grace* gave it to Abraham through a promise" (NIV).
Ephesians 2:5	"By *grace* you have been saved" (NKJV).
Ephesians 2:8	"For by *grace* you have been saved through faith, and this is not your own doing; it is the gift of God" (NRSV).
2 Timothy 1:9	"Who has saved us and called us to a holy life—not because of anything we have done but because of his own purpose and *grace*. This *grace* was given us in Christ Jesus before the beginning of time" (NIV).
Titus 3:4-7	"But when the kindness and love of God our Savior appeared, he saved us, not because of righteous things we had done, but because of his mercy. He saved us . . . so that, having been justified by his *grace,* we might become heirs having the hope of eternal life" (NIV).

2:10 For we are God's workmanship, created in Christ Jesus to do good works, which God prepared in advance for us to do.^{NIV} But wait, there's more. *We are God's workmanship* (work of art, masterpiece, new creation). Salvation is something only God can do—it is his powerful, creative work in us. People are re-created into new people, and those new people form a new creation—the church.

The verb "created" is used only of God—for only God can truly create. As he created the universe from nothing, so he creates new, alive, spiritual beings from the old, dead, sinful creatures we were— "So if anyone is in Christ, there is a new creation: everything old has passed away; see, everything has become new!" (2 Corinthians 5:17 NRSV). Then God forms believers into a unified body, his church (see 2:15; 4:24; Colossians 3:10). *In Christ Jesus* emphasizes the source of this creation, as in 2:6-7—Christ has provided salvation.

GOD'S MASTERPIECES
Why would God do it? Why would he sacrifice his only Son for sinners like us? Ephesians 2:10 gives one reason: so that we could be living, breathing pictures of his grace and mercy. Not only does he change us radically into new creatures, he also wants to use us as display cases for his artistry. According to this verse, believers are his workmanship, his masterpieces. That would be an arrogant claim to make about ourselves if God hadn't already said it. This statement also carries some significant implications about how we ought to see ourselves and how we ought to treat one another. God's masterpieces should not lower or degrade themselves with sinful attitudes, words, or behaviors. Nor should we devalue his other works of art: our brothers and sisters in Christ. Treat fellow Christians as God's masterpieces.

That we are God's "workmanship" may be intended as a contrast leading into *good works*. God's "work" of salvation and new creation overturns our "sinful works" and makes doing "good works" possible. People become Christians through God's undeserved favor (his grace), not as the result of any efforts, abilities, intelligent choices, personal characteristics, or acts of service. Out of gratitude for this free gift, however, believers will seek "to do good works"—to help and serve others with kindness, love, and gentleness. While no action or work we do can help us obtain salvation, God's intention is that our salvation will result in acts of service. We are saved not merely for our own benefit but to serve Christ and build up the church

(4:12). This solves the so-called conflict between faith and works. Works do not produce salvation but are the evidence of salvation (see James 1:22; 2:14-26).

The Greek word translated "do" *(peripateo)* means "to walk about in." We move ahead in this life of grace doing the good works *which God prepared in advance for us to do.* The new life that God gives cannot help but express itself in good works. This does not necessarily mean that God has set up all the specific good works each person will do—although there would be no point arguing against the possibility of our omniscient God doing just that. Just as God planned salvation in Jesus Christ before the foundation of the world, so he planned that believers should do good to others (see 1 Timothy 6:18; Titus 2:7; 1 Peter 2:12).

CHRIST IS THE WAY TO PEACE / 2:11-22

Before Christ's coming, Gentiles and Jews kept apart from one another. Jews considered Gentiles beyond God's saving power and therefore without hope. Gentiles resented Jewish claims of their position of superiority based on their heritage. Christ revealed the total sinfulness of both Jews and Gentiles, and then he offered his salvation to both. Only Christ breaks down the walls of prejudice, reconciles all believers to God, and unifies us in one body.

2:11 Therefore, remember that formerly you who are Gentiles by birth and called "uncircumcised" by those who call themselves "the circumcision" (that done in the body by the hands of men).NIV Christ Jesus set individuals free from sin and death by making them alive through faith in him (2:1-10), but there is more to the story. Jesus saved individuals of all races and backgrounds in order to bring them into unity as his body, his church. There existed a huge gulf between Jews and Gentiles (non-Jews). God was going to bring these two distinct groups together by drawing believers in Christ from among the Jews *and* from among the Gentiles.

The Jews had the privilege of being God's chosen nation to whom he had given his covenant promises (Deuteronomy 7:6). One of the signs of his covenant was circumcision. God required circumcision:

- As a sign of obedience to him.
- As a sign of belonging to his covenant people, because once circumcised, the man would be identified as a Jew forever.
- As a symbol of "cutting off" the old life of sin, purifying one's

heart, and dedicating oneself to God. More than any other practice, circumcision separated God's people from their Egyptian and Canaanite neighbors.

Pious Jews ("the circumcision") considered all non-Jews (the "uncircumcised") to be ceremonially unclean. The Jews erred in believing that circumcision *(that done in the body by the hands of men)* was sufficient to make them godly without the necessity of inner renewal (see Paul's discussion of this in Romans 2:25-29; also see Galatians 5:6). In this section in Ephesians, Paul focused on the Gentiles, calling the Gentile Christians to *remember* their former condition. "Remember" in the Bible means more than mere recollection; it is a call to action on the basis of the memory (Exodus 12:14; 1 Corinthians 11:25).

2:12 Remember that at that time you were separate from Christ, excluded from citizenship in Israel and foreigners to the covenants of the promise, without hope and without God in the world.NIV Compared to the Jews, the Gentiles had five distinct disadvantages:

1. They were *separate from Christ,* having had no expectation of a Messiah to save them.
2. They were *excluded from citizenship in Israel.* Gentiles could never fully partake of the spiritual privileges promised to Israel, God's chosen people. While Gentiles could become Jews after an extensive training period, followed by circumcision and baptism, the sense of "exclusion" was never fully removed. Gentiles could never truly be citizens of Israel.
3. They were *foreigners to the covenants of the promise.* For Paul, the covenant promises were the basis for Israel's distinctive. The plural ("covenants") makes the word comprehensive—all of God's promises to his people, all the distinctive privileges that made them his people. To these, the Gentiles were "foreigners," meaning that they had no share or part in the promises.
4. They were *without hope.* There was no hope for the Gentiles to find the one true God or to obtain anything beyond physical life in this world. The pagan philosophers' theories about life after death were at best vague and supplied no way to atone for evil committed during a person's life. They had no "divine promise" and, thus, no basis for hope.
5. They were *without God in the world.* The Gentiles had many gods, but they were without the one true God. They lived entirely and only in this evil world. Without God, the world was all they had.

This was a bleak description indeed. Fortunately, it does not end here, for God himself intervened.

REMEMBER THE WAY YOU WERE
History is filled with stories of groups who hated one another for various reasons. In American folklore, we have the Hatfields and McCoys; in Ireland, it's the Protestants versus the Catholics. In Bosnia, it's the Serbs versus the Croats. There was no love lost between first-century Jews and Gentiles, either. The Jews considered the Gentiles little better than animals, and the Gentiles resented the Jews for their smug religious superiority. But here in Ephesians, Paul told the Gentile Christians to remember what it felt like to be treated that way, to be seen as unworthy outsiders . . . and he told them *not* to return the favor. He called on them to remember where (and *what*) they were when God found them: separated from Christ, excluded from his promises, without hope and without God. A bleak picture indeed—but God changed all that by his mercy. Therefore, all Christians (including *us*) should extend that grace to others, even former antagonists. Think what would happen to conflicts in the church—conflicts over money, race, music, personality, etc.—if we took Paul's admonition to heart. Let it start with you.

2:13 But now in Christ Jesus you who once were far off have been brought near by the blood of Christ.[NKJV] The two little words "but now" reveal God's intervention from heaven to earth and the entire story of redemption. Contrasting the Gentiles' state "at that time" (2:12, that is, before they knew Christ), this passage describes the joyous reconciliation that the Gentile believers have experienced *in Christ Jesus*. "Jesus" was added to the title "Christ" used in 2:12, implying that he is not only the Jewish Messiah but also the Savior of the world.

The words "far" and "near" describe the position of Gentiles and Jews in relation to God. Isaiah spoke of a coming day of "peace, to those far and near" (Isaiah 57:19 NIV). To accomplish this "peace" and to "bring near" those who had been far away could only happen *by the blood of Christ*. Redemption could come only through Jesus' death. "Without the shedding of blood there is no forgiveness" (Hebrews 9:22 NIV). For more about why Jesus had to die, see commentary on 1:7-8.

2:14 For he is our peace; in his flesh he has made both groups into one and has broken down the dividing wall, that is, the hostility between us.[NRSV] Christ Jesus, through his death *(in his flesh)*, destroyed the barriers that had separated Jews and Gentiles, making peace between *both groups*. This, in turn, made the way for peace between them. Even more than making peace between the two groups, Christ reconciled them both to God. Those who believed in him would be made *into one* group, Christians, where "there is no Greek or Jew, circumcised or uncircumcised, barbarian, Scythian, slave or free, but Christ is all, and is in all" (Colossians 3:11 NIV; see also Galatians 3:28).

AND
Christ's sacrifice atoned for the sins of all kinds of people—Jews *and* Gentiles. Jews and Gentiles alike could be guilty of spiritual pride—Jews for thinking that their faith and traditions elevated them above everyone else, Gentiles for trusting in their achievements, power, or position. Spiritual pride blinds us to our own faults and magnifies the faults of others. Be careful not to become proud of your salvation. Instead, humbly thank God for what he has done, and encourage others who might be struggling in their faith.

In addition to bringing peace to individuals and between people, Christ himself *is our peace.* The prophet Micah wrote, "This One shall be peace," (Micah 5:5 NKJV), and Isaiah prophesied the coming of the Prince of Peace (Isaiah 9:6). Unfortunately, this peace that Christ made between the two groups has not been the practical experience of Gentiles and Jews throughout the years. The requirement for peace for both as defined here would be faith in Christ.

Paul described the peace that Christ had made between Jews and Gentiles as a *dividing wall* that had been *broken down.* It was no secret that *hostility* (also translated "enmity") existed between the two groups, a cultural and religious hostility that no one could bridge—no one but God. This "dividing wall" alludes to the wall in the Jewish temple that separated the court of the Gentiles from the temple proper, which only Jews could enter. The Jewish historian Josephus wrote that on this wall was an inscription in Greek and Latin: "No foreigner may enter within the barricade that surrounds the sanctuary and enclosure. Anyone who is caught doing so will have himself to blame for his ensuing death" (see Acts 21:28-29). Christ did not literally break down the wall; it was destroyed when the temple was destroyed in A.D. 70. This "breaking down" refers symbolically to Christ's reconciliation.

2:15-16 **He has abolished the law with its commandments and ordinances, that he might create in himself one new humanity in place of the two, thus making peace, and might reconcile both groups to God in one body through the cross, thus putting to**

death that hostility through it.[NRSV] The "dividing wall" (2:14)
was also pictured in the Jewish law itself, for the *law* was the
means by which the Jews justified themselves before God and
excluded the Gentiles (Deuteronomy 31:11-13; Isaiah 51:7-8).
Christ himself said that he did not come to abolish the law but to
fulfill it (Matthew 5:17). Christ fulfilled the Old Testament law
because that law (especially the ceremonial law with its regula-
tions for sacrifices) foreshadowed his coming. In his life on earth,
he obeyed and supported the intent of the law as God's revelation
and standard for people's behavior (see Matthew 5:21-48). Paul
also supports the moral and ethical purpose of the law as valid to
guide us (Romans 3:19-31; Galatians 3:24). But in his death and
resurrection, Jesus annulled the law—that is, he made it ineffec-
tive. The law was annulled because of its ineffectiveness to make
people right with God.

The demands of the law were intended to make people see
their inability to be "good enough" apart from Christ (Romans
3:19-20; 7:7-13). No one could perfectly keep the law *with its
commandments and ordinances,* so Christ *has abolished the law*
by perfectly fulfilling it.

All have sinned; neither Gentiles *nor* Jews are capable of keeping God's law. All need a Savior. That Savior came, died, and
rose again, fulfilling and abolishing the law as the way of salvation. Jesus then opened to both Jews and Gentiles a way to God
by faith in him (John 14:6). By offering salvation to all kinds of
people, Christ could *create in himself one new humanity in place
of the two.* In Christ there are no longer Jews and Gentiles but a
mixture of Jews and Gentiles, combined as Christians, who make
up the body of which he is the Head. By doing so, Christ also
could *reconcile both groups to God in one body*—that is, in the
church. This reconciliation could occur only *through the cross*
because Jesus' death was the substitutionary sacrifice fulfilling
the demands of the law, taking its punishment in our place. Not
only were Jews and Gentiles reconciled to God, but they were
also reconciled to each other, for Jesus' death on the cross put *to
death* any remaining *hostility* between them. There was no necessity for further hostility other than their refusal to accept Christ's
reconciliation.

Because Christ broke down the dividing wall, believing Jews
and Gentiles can have unity with one another in Christ. Because
of Christ's death, believers are one (2:14); we are reconciled to
one another (2:16); we have access to the Father by the Holy
Spirit (2:18); we are no longer foreigners or aliens to God (2:19);

we are all being built into a holy temple with Christ as our chief cornerstone (2:20-21).

BARRIER BREAKERS
Christianity is the only religion in the world that can truly be described as an equal-opportunity faith. All Christians stand on level ground before the cross of Christ: young and old, male and female, Jew and Gentile, rich and poor, and black, white, and every other color. We are all sinners in need of salvation. Other religions set up barriers between people. Hindus believe in a caste system; Muslim men will not worship with Muslim women; until very recently, black people could not join the Mormon church. Christ alone abolishes all these barriers. Are there barriers in your church (or in your heart) based on race, economics, or sex? Check your attitudes and actions against Scripture. If you find yourself out of accord with it, repent and ask God to help you. Don't put up walls where Christ has torn them down.

2:17 **And He came and preached peace to you who were afar off and to those who were near.**^{NKJV} Continuing the theme of 2:14-16, this *peace* preached by Christ includes peace with God and peace between Jews (the chosen people, *those who were near*) and Gentiles (those *who were afar off* and without God, 2:12). In these words, Paul may have been alluding to Isaiah 52:7 and Isaiah 57:19. According to the sequence of the previous verses, this coming to preach was (1) Jesus' coming after the Resurrection to preach to the apostles directly (see Luke 24:36; John 20:19, 21, 26); and (2) Jesus' coming through the Spirit to preach to all people. The Jews were *near* to God because they already knew of him through the Scriptures and worshiped him in their religious ceremonies. The Gentiles were *afar off* because they knew little or nothing about God. Because neither group could be saved by good deeds, knowledge, or sincerity, both needed to hear about the salvation available through Jesus Christ. Both Jews and Gentiles are now free to come to God through Christ.

2:18 **For through Him we both have access by one Spirit to the Father.**^{NKJV} It is only *through Him* (through Jesus' sacrifice on the cross) that *we both have access . . . to the Father.* "Both" (referring to believing Jews and Gentiles) are united in *one Spirit.* The word "access" pictures being presented to a king in his throne room. Through Christ, the believer is ushered into God's very presence (see 3:12). The One we come to see is not

only the King but "the Father"—the One who has adopted us as
his very own children (Romans 8:15; Galatians 4:6).

PEACEMAKERS
Christ brought the gospel to all races of people. Christianity
is open to all, regardless of race, ethnic background, and
economic status, so it shouldn't surprise us if there are some
adjustment problems in making all these different kinds of
people into one body. After all, Jews and Gentiles had spent
centuries developing a deep animosity toward one another. It
could hardly be expected to evaporate at once. In fact, you
wouldn't expect it to disappear at all—unless something other
than human nature was at work. Something *was,* and *is:* the
peace of God, which is far beyond human comprehension.
Christ, the Prince of Peace, has called us to peace as well.
Peace with God and peace with one another. Can you describe
your relationships with others in the body as characterized by
peace? If so, thank God, who alone makes it possible. If not,
repent and ask God to give you grace to make those relationships right.

Christ provides the access to the Father by one Spirit (the Holy
Spirit), who helps us when we pray (Romans 8:26-27) and who
baptizes and unifies us into one body (1 Corinthians 12:13). Note
the three distinct persons of the Trinity mentioned in this verse.
All people have direct access to God through Christ by means of
the Holy Spirit. This "access" refers to God's presence and power
as well as to the blessings of his kingdom. Because of Christ, all
believers can "come boldly to the throne of grace" (Hebrews
4:16 NKJV).

**2:19 Consequently, you are no longer foreigners and aliens, but
fellow citizens with God's people and members of God's
household.**NIV The Gentiles *are no longer foreigners and
aliens.* These words describe people who live in a country other
than their own without any of the rights of citizenship in that
country. The Gentiles were "outsiders" in relation to the Jews,
as well as to any hope (without Christ) for a relationship with
God (2:12). That was their old position. Because of Christ,
however, the Gentiles became *fellow citizens* with all who have
been called to be *God's people.* Jews and Gentiles who put
their faith in Jesus Christ as their Savior become *members of
God's household,* that is, God's family. (See Philippians 3:20;
Hebrews 3:2-6)

All believers are citizens of God's kingdom and members of
his household. Many barriers divide us from other Christians:

age, appearance, intelligence, political persuasion, economic status, race, theological perspective. One of the surest ways to stifle Christ's love is to be friendly only with those people who are similar to us. Fortunately, Christ has knocked down the barriers and has placed all believers into one family. His cross should be the focus of our unity. The Holy Spirit helps us look beyond the barriers to the unity we are called to enjoy. People can see that God is love and that Christ is Lord as we live in harmony with each other and in accordance with what God says in his Word.

> Sovereign grace can make strangers into sons.
> *C. H. Spurgeon*

THE CITIZEN
Imagine that you are a refugee from another country. After surviving your flight to this country, destitute and homeless, you want to become a citizen. Imagine further that after taking the oath of allegiance, the judge who authorizes your citizenship invites you to come live in his palatial home along with a number of other immigrants. Would you accept his generous offer? Of course! Once there, would you be grateful, or would you take it upon yourself to complain about your accommodations and fellow occupants? The answer should be obvious, and so should the analogy. God, in his mercy, has taken us—foreigners and aliens—and made us part of his kingdom and even members of his own household. What kind of lives should he then expect from us: critical, complaining, argumentative, never satisfied? No! Our lives should be characterized by gratitude, patience with one another, and praise for God's benevolence.

2:20 Having been built on the foundation of the apostles and prophets, Jesus Christ Himself being the chief cornerstone.[NKJV] God's "household" (2:19) is built on a solid foundation, *the foundation of the apostles and prophets.* Paul used a common metaphor to describe Christ—the *chief cornerstone.* This alludes to Psalm 118:22 and Isaiah 8:14; 28:16 (see also Romans 9:32-33; 1 Peter 2:4-8). Paul expanded the metaphor, describing the apostles and prophets as the "foundation." Every well-built structure with a firm foundation has a cornerstone. A cornerstone is a valued architectural piece. Stonemasons choose just the right rock. The cornerstone anchors the building and gives all the walls their line. Jesus is the chief cornerstone of God's building. The "prophets" here are probably the New Testament prophets (see 3:5; 4:11) because "apostles" are listed first. These apostles and prophets received and believed in Jesus Christ as their Messiah; then they took the gospel message out to the world.

2:21 In him the whole building is joined together and rises to become a holy temple in the Lord.^{NIV} The body of believers, the church, was *joined together* and continues to rise (or grow) *in him,* that is, in Christ. In Greek there is no definite article *(the)* so this "building" may refer both to a structure (with Christ as cornerstone, 2:20) and to the building process. Each part of the building, each believer, fits perfectly into the building, all the pieces being aligned with the Cornerstone. The structure is not yet complete; it will not be complete until the day that Christ Jesus returns. The building's purpose is also described: *to become a holy temple in the Lord.* The church becomes a holy temple because of the presence of the holy God. The word used for "temple" here refers to what was the inner sanctuary (the Most Holy Place) in the Jewish temple. The union of God with people, and the unity of previously alienated people with one another, could only occur *in the Lord.*

> There is a sense in which the people of the Lord are a people apart, belonging to each other in a sense in which they don't belong to anyone else.
> *A. W. Tozer*

CLEAN HOUSE

If the president were coming to visit you—or perhaps a king or queen—what would you do? Straighten up the house, mow the lawn, and trim the shrubs? No doubt you would do all that and more. When we belong to Christ, the King of kings and Lord of lords, he doesn't just come to visit. He takes up residence in our hearts. We are his dwelling place, both individually as believers and collectively as the church. Since we are together a living, growing holy temple, a dwelling in which God lives by his Spirit, what kind of dwelling place ought we to be? One marked by factions, divisions, self-seeking, quarrels over money and worship styles? Or one that exudes unity, servanthood, joy, self-sacrifice, and love? In which place would you rather live?

2:22 And in him you too are being built together to become a dwelling in which God lives by his Spirit.^{NIV} *In him* (in Christ) *you too* (Gentile believers) are joined with Jewish believers *to become* an entirely new kind of *dwelling,* a dwelling described in 2:19-21. In the Old Testament, God's "dwelling" referred either to the nation of Israel or to the tabernacle or temple. But in the New Testament, this *dwelling* is the whole body of believers, the church, made up of both Jews and Gentiles. There would not be two "churches"—one made up of Jewish believers and one of Gentile believers (as almost happened in the early church). Believers are *being built together* in Christ, so there should be no barriers, no divisions, no basis for discrimination. We all belong to Christ and share fully in his blessings. He lives in us (corporately and individually) *by his Spirit,* the Holy Spirit.

Ephesians 3

3:1 For this reason I, Paul, the prisoner of Christ Jesus for the sake of you Gentiles.[NIV] The words "for this reason" refer back to 2:22 and probably to all that Paul had explained in 2:11-22. Paul had been arrested in Jerusalem and, eventually, had been imprisoned because he took a stand for the equality of Jews and Gentiles as Christians (believers in Christ). The Jewish antagonists saw Paul's teaching as radical and destructive to temple practices. Thus, Paul was writing here that he had been imprisoned *for the sake of you Gentiles.* The religious leaders in Jerusalem, who felt scandalized by Jesus' teachings and didn't believe he was the Messiah, pressured the Romans to arrest Paul and bring him to trial for treason and for causing rebellion among the Jews. They used Trophimus, the Ephesian Gentile convert, as a ploy to arrest Paul. Paul had appealed for his case to be heard by the emperor, and he was awaiting trial (see Acts 21:21, 28; 28:16-31). Yet Paul knew that his imprisonment was by God's will—therefore, he called himself *the prisoner of Christ Jesus*—not of the Jews, not of the Romans, but of Christ Jesus himself (see Ephesians 4:1; Philippians 1:1; 2 Timothy 1:8).

Verses 2-13 are a parenthesis; then Paul repeats the words "for this reason" in 3:14 and continues with the verb ("I kneel"), finishing the thought begun here.

IN GOD'S HANDS
The noted psychotherapist Viktor Frankl maintained that people can endure any "what" as long as they have a "why." He spoke with credibility—he had survived the Holocaust. Paul suffered greatly for his outspoken faith in Jesus (see 2 Corinthians 11:23-33), referring to himself as "the prisoner of Christ Jesus for the sake of you Gentiles." How could Paul persevere in the face of such suffering? He had a "why" for the "what." Paul knew that his life was in God's hands and that nothing had come into his life that had not first passed through nail-scarred hands. Do you have that confidence? Regard your circumstances as the proving ground of God's great mercy and love.

3:2-3 Surely you have heard about the administration of God's grace that was given to me for you, that is, the mystery made known to me by revelation, as I have already written briefly.[NIV] Digressing slightly from the thought he had begun in 3:1 (he completes the thought in 3:14), Paul explained more fully his ministry to the Gentiles. The words "surely you have heard" are rhetorical; Paul assumed that the Ephesians and the believers in surrounding cities knew *about the administration of God's grace that was given* to him on their (the Gentiles') behalf. "The administration of God's grace" means the special stewardship, trust, or commission that Paul had been given, and the grace and authority he had been given in order to fulfill it (see 3:9). *For you* indicates that God had given Paul this special stewardship for the sake of others, not just for Paul's own benefit. God had assigned to Paul the special work of preaching the Good News to the Gentiles (Acts 9:15). The Greek word translated "administration" is *oikonomia,* usually referring to household management. This continues the image of God's "household" from 2:19-22.

FOR OTHERS
Have you ever considered the fact that everything God gives us as abilities, spiritual gifts, and opportunities for ministry are for the sake of others? After all, if salvation were just for our benefit, God could simply take us to heaven as soon as we believed and give us the greatest blessing of all, eternity with him. The reason he keeps us here is for us to be his agents, his representatives to others. All that we have is a sacred stewardship from him. Just as Jesus laid down his life for us, so we should serve others in his name. What has God given you—and your church—in terms of spiritual gifts, material wealth, and service opportunities? What specifically are you doing with it? What kind of steward are you?

That the Gentiles could be included in God's grace is called a mystery (Paul described this amazing new truth at length in 2:11-22). This "mystery" was a plan at one time hidden but now revealed (see 1:9). The mystery was hidden, not because only a few could understand it, but because it was hidden until Christ came. God had made this mystery known to Paul *by revelation.* A "revelation" is a direct communication from God. Paul had refused to believe in Christ and had persecuted anyone who did (Acts 9:1-2). God got hold of Paul and *made known* to him, through personal revelation, that Jesus Christ truly was the promised Messiah of the Jews and the light to the Gentiles, too. Both Jews and Gentiles would be included in the church. "As I have already written briefly" most likely refers to earlier parts of this

letter, rather than to another unpreserved letter. The next verse
makes this clear.

**3:4 In reading this, then, you will be able to understand my insight
into the mystery of Christ.**^{NIV} When a church received a letter
from Paul or one of the other apostles (such as the letters from
Peter, James, and Jude), a church leader would read the letter aloud
to the assembled congregation. Paul wrote to this leader and to the
congregation, explaining that *in reading* (or hearing) the letter, they
would *be able to understand* his *insight into the mystery of Christ.*
The word "this" probably refers to Paul's words in the earlier chapters of this letter explaining the mystery, as well as to his words in
3:3. Why did Paul have such insight into this mystery of Christ, and
how could he explain it so clearly? Because it had been revealed to
him by God himself!

The "mystery of Christ" means "the mystery about Christ" or
"the mystery, the substance of which is Christ." In Colossians 1:27,
the mystery is the indwelling Christ, "Christ in you, the hope of
glory." In Ephesians 1:9, the mystery refers to God's plan to unite
all creation in Christ. Here in Ephesians 3:6, the mystery refers to
the fact that Jews and Gentiles who believe are united in Christ.

**3:5 In former generations this mystery was not made known to
humankind, as it has now been revealed to his holy apostles
and prophets by the Spirit.**^{NRSV} God's method of communicating with the Israelites was to reveal his words to a chosen
prophet, who would in turn teach the people. The *former generations* in the time of the Old Testament prophets did not clearly
understand the *mystery* which *has now been revealed to his holy
apostles and prophets by the Spirit.* God's plan was hidden from
previous generations, not because God wanted to keep something
from his people, but because he would reveal it to everyone in
his perfect timing (see also Colossians 1:25-26). God planned to
have Jews and Gentiles comprise one body, the church. These
"prophets" are New Testament prophets (see also 2:20; 4:11).
The phrase "by the Spirit" focuses on divine revelation and inspiration. The revealing of this mystery to one of the *holy apostles* is
recorded in Acts 10. Peter received a dream making clear to him
that the gospel message was meant not for the Jews alone but
also for Gentiles. Peter followed God's guidance, so Cornelius, a
Roman centurion, and his household became believers, received
the Holy Spirit, and were baptized. Likewise Paul had received a
message: "The following night the Lord stood near Paul and said,
'Take courage! As you have testified about me in Jerusalem, so
you must also testify in Rome'" (Acts 23:11 NIV).

3:6 This mystery is that through the gospel the Gentiles are heirs together with Israel, members together of one body, and sharers together in the promise in Christ Jesus.[NIV] In case anyone missed his point, Paul explained exactly what that *mystery* entailed. While the early prophets had written of the inclusion of Gentiles with Jews (see, for example, Isaiah 49:6; 56:6-7;), their writings were interpreted that the Gentiles could become prose-lytes. The extent of this inclusion and the radical change—the Jews and Gentiles becoming one body under Christ's head-ship—was not even considered. No one ever knew this until God revealed it to Paul and the other New Testament apostles and proph-ets. This inclusion of Gentiles with Jews is described in three terms:

> When we take God for our God, we take his people for our people.
> *Matthew Henry*

1. *Heirs together*—As "heirs" together, Jews and Gentiles are adopted into the same family, thus becoming brothers and sisters. Gentiles are fellow heirs of salvation and share equally with the Jews (Romans 8:17; Galatians 3:29; 4:7).
2. *Members together*—As "members . . . of one body," they are united into one unit under Christ, the Head. Paul used the word *sus-soma* (cobody). This was never used in Greek literature before Paul.
3. *Sharers together*—As "sharers . . . in the promise," they will be fellow partakers and copartners in receiving the coming blessings promised in God's kingdom (2 Timothy 1:1).

ONE BODY
Can churches be truly united? You have heard that opposites attract. That can be true, but often our churches are exceptions. It is a sad truth that the church remains one of the most segre-gated entities left in our culture. Paul would have been not only saddened by this, he probably also would have been shocked. After all, God had used Paul more than anyone else to proclaim the unified nature of the body of Christ, a unity that would bring together even Jews and Gentiles (no groups then or now had any greater animosity toward one another). If God could bring them together, he can unite anyone. Paul calls us to take an honest look at our relationships with Christians of other races and ethnic backgrounds. Do you have any real friendships that reach beyond racial barriers? Does your church? What are you doing to further manifest God's "revealed mystery," the reconciliation of all racial and ethnic groups into one body, *his* body, the church?

This unity occurs *through the gospel* message when they believe. This unity transcends race, culture, gender, age, and any other factor that divides people. Only *in Christ Jesus* could such unity be possible.

OUR LIVES BEFORE AND AFTER CHRIST

BEFORE	AFTER
Dead in transgressions.	Made alive with Christ
Objects of wrath.	Shown God's mercy and given salvation
Followed the ways of the world	Stand for Christ and truth
God's enemies.	God's children
Enslaved to Satan	Free in Christ to love and serve him

3:7 I became a servant of this gospel by the gift of God's grace given me through the working of his power.[NIV] The unity Paul described above can only happen when the gospel message is preached and believed. *This gospel* refers to the message of Jesus Christ as Messiah and Savior of all who believe—whether Jews or Gentiles. Paul *became* (literally "was made" or "created") *a servant* of this gospel. (The word for "minister," *diakonos,* refers to a servant but one who held that office in the church. This is different from the word *doulos* meaning "slave.") Paul did not seek this job description, nor was it given to him on the basis of earned degree or merit.

Paul explained that his servanthood was *by the gift of God's grace given . . . through the working of his power.* Paul had actually been working for the "other side" when God called him—Paul had rejected Jesus as the Messiah and had actively persecuted Christians. Obviously God had not called Paul on the basis of his goodness or apparent faithfulness! God made Paul a key messenger of the gospel in the early days of the church. Yet Paul realized that he could not have fulfilled this mission without God's grace and power within him.

OPPORTUNITIES
When Paul became a servant of the gospel, God gave him the ability to share the gospel of Christ effectively. You may not be an apostle or even an evangelist, but God will give you opportunities to tell others about Christ. And with the opportunities he will provide the ability, courage, and power. Make yourself available to God as his servant whenever an opportunity presents itself. As you focus on the other person and his or her needs, God will communicate your caring attitude. Your words will be natural, loving, and compelling.

God in his grace gave Paul the gift of salvation. Grace and salvation lead to a life filled with God's power and working for God's kingdom. Only God's grace and power could accomplish such a change in Paul's life.

> There is no pit so deep that Jesus is not deeper still.
> *Corrie ten Boom*

3:8 To me, who am less than the least of all the saints, this grace was given, that I should preach among the Gentiles the unsearchable riches of Christ.NKJV When Paul described himself as *less than the least of all the saints,* he meant that God's grace alone had saved him, the one who had hated and persecuted all who followed Jesus. Nothing in Paul merited such grace; Paul knew this and was utterly amazed at what God had done. God had chosen him and had saved him. "This grace" refers to the special calling that God had given to Paul—that he *should preach among the Gentiles.* The word "preach" was deliberately chosen by the early church to refer to the proclamation of the gospel. Paul considered telling others about Christ to be like sharing *unsearchable riches.* "Unsearchable" means that the wonder of God's grace exceeds the frontiers of our ability to understand. To the Gentiles, who had been excluded by the Jews from participation in God's kingdom (2:12-13), these riches were unfathomable.

3:9 And to make plain to everyone the administration of this mystery, which for ages past was kept hidden in God, who created all things.NIV Paul's job was *to make plain to everyone the administration of this mystery* (see 3:2). All people were to know that it pleased God at this time to make known or bring to light his secret plan (explained in 3:6). The "administration" or "carrying out" of this explanation of the mystery occurred as Paul and the other apostles taught God's great purpose in Christ and as the church itself took root and grew. For Paul, "making plain" God's mystery was at the core of his selection as an apostle. Paul understood that he was born at a specific time to fulfill a specific purpose—revealing this mystery that *for ages past was kept hidden in God.* God knew the plan all along but had kept it a secret until the appropriate time. God, *who created all things,* was at work both in the former creation and the new creation. The same God is at work, and his plan was in place before the creation of the world.

> We have not merely been saved that we might escape hell; we have been saved in order that God may present a people which will astonish the whole world.
> *Dr. Martyn Lloyd-Jones*

3:10 So that through the church the wisdom of God in its rich variety might now be made known to the rulers and authorities in the heavenly places.^{NRSV} God's mystery was to build a church by uniting Jews and Gentiles as believers in Jesus Christ. *Through* this joining of believers in *the church, the wisdom of God in its rich variety* (God's "manifold wisdom") will be powerfully displayed. This wisdom will *be made known to the rulers and authorities in the heavenly places.* Paul had written in 2:7 that "in the ages to come" Christ would "show the exceeding riches of His grace," hinting that God's purpose for the church is not limited by time or space. Even the angels would see the mystery unfold. (See also 1:21-22 and commentary there.)

In this verse, "rulers and authorities" refers to both good and evil angels. (In 1:21, the words referred to angelic powers; in 6:12, they refer to demonic powers.) All powers in the heavenlies, whether evil or good, will receive their understanding of God's great mystery from humans. God builds his church on earth from saved sinners, who, through God's grace and mercy, received their salvation through Jesus Christ's death on the cross. No angel or demon can comprehend what God has done.

3:11 According to the eternal purpose which He accomplished in Christ Jesus our Lord.^{NKJV} God, "who created all things" (3:9), has always been in control of his creation. The plan of salvation, the mystery of the church, and the revelation of his wisdom across all the realms of creation will occur *according to the eternal purpose.* God's plan did not arise as an emergency measure when Adam sinned; it did not occur because God somehow lost control. God has always been in control, and his eternal purposes will always be accomplished. The central theme of this letter is God's great work of joining Jews and Gentiles together in a unified body—the church. God could only accept sinful people through a sacrifice that would cover their sins. Jesus Christ gave that sacrifice—himself—through his death on the cross. *In Christ Jesus our Lord,* God *accomplished* the plan he had prepared before the world began.

3:12 In him and through faith in him we may approach God with freedom and confidence.^{NIV} God accomplished his eternal plan by sending his Son to die on a cross as a sacrifice for sin. Only *in* Christ and *through faith* in Christ are people able to approach the holy God. Paul described the most awesome privilege any mere human could have—to be able to *approach God with freedom and confidence.* Most of us would be apprehensive in the presence of a powerful ruler, but faith gives us confidence. The Greek word translated "approach" implies a formal introduction into the presence of a king. Thanks to Jesus Christ, Christians can enter directly into God's presence through prayer (see also Hebrews 4:16; 10:19-22).

OPEN INVITATION
Suppose you were touring the White House one day and the president himself made an unexpected appearance with your group. You barely have time to regain your composure when he walks straight over to you and says, "I'm free tonight; you want to come back and have dinner?" You would probably find the time to make the return trip. Through Christ, we are given access not to any earthly king or head of state but to God Almighty. And not just *occasional* access when we have something really heavy on our minds. Instead, we have total, constant access to approach God "with freedom and confidence." Take God up on his gracious offer.

3:13 **I ask you, therefore, not to be discouraged because of my sufferings for you, which are your glory.**[NIV] *Therefore,* because of the tremendous scope of God's plan and because God gave believers access to him in freedom and confidence (3:12), Paul asked his readers *not to be discouraged* because of his *sufferings.* Paul had been imprisoned for championing the ministry of the gospel to the Gentiles (Acts 21:27-36). He could truly say to these Gentile believers that his sufferings were *for you,* but he asked that they not be discouraged. Instead, they should regard them as *glory.* Why should Paul's suffering make the Ephesians feel honored? If Paul had not preached the gospel, he would not be in jail—but then the Ephesians might not have heard the Good News and been converted. Just as a mother endures the pain of childbirth in order to bring new life into the world, Paul endured the pain of persecution in order to bring new believers to Christ. Obeying Christ is never easy. He requires you to take up your cross and follow him (Matthew 16:24). That means being willing to endure pain so that God's message of salvation can reach the entire world. We should feel honored that others have suffered and sacrificed for us so that we might reap the benefit. Because he understood that the Creator God was completely in control, Paul also understood that God was working his will even through his imprisonment and suffering. In this, the Ephesian believers could "glory."

THE MAGNITUDE OF GOD'S LOVE / 3:14-21

Paul's prayer for the Ephesians is that they be united by the Spirit, indwelt by Christ, and filled with all the fullness of God's love.

**3:14-15 For this reason I bow my knees before the Father, from whom
every family in heaven and on earth takes its name.**NRSV The
phrase "for this reason" actually continues the thought begun in
3:1. There Paul had said "for this reason," referring back to his
words in 2:11-22 regarding the union of Jews and Gentiles. Over-
whelmed by the blessings given to Jews and Gentiles and the
privilege of sharing this newly revealed "mystery," Paul exclaimed,
I bow my knees before the Father. The following words are his
prayer for the Ephesians. While it was common among Jews to
stand in prayer, kneeling revealed the earnestness and humble submission that Paul felt as he spoke these words (see Luke 22:41;
Acts 7:60; 9:40; 20:36).

The phrase "every family in heaven and on earth" refers to all
powers—visible and invisible (3:10). These "families" are the
basic relationship structures that exist. "Takes its name" refers to
a practice in ancient days where a name would reveal one's basic
character. God as "the Father" is the Creator and Redeemer—
through these words, Paul praised God's "fatherhood" over us all.
God is in complete control of his creation. When his children
kneel before him in prayer, they come to the God who is in complete and ultimate control. These words set the tone for the prayer
that follows.

HEART AND KNEE
In the preceding verses, Paul touched on a number of themes
that could elicit different responses from his readers—pride,
fear, smugness, gratitude. Paul's own response, however, to
what God had done with him and through him, was to kneel
before God in humility and adoration. How do you respond to
the "highs and lows" of your Christian walk? Do you get ecstatic
over good events and depressed over the bad? Learn a lesson
from Paul, who experienced highs of grace and glory and lows
of suffering and loss. Meet all your circumstances with humility,
and trust in God's sovereign goodness, with bended knee and
yielded heart.

**3:16 I pray that, according to the riches of his glory, he may grant
that you may be strengthened in your inner being with power
through his Spirit.**NRSV This beautiful prayer for the Ephesian
believers (3:16-21) includes some of the most loved verses in
the New Testament. Paul knelt before the Father (3:14); then he
prayed that God would *grant* certain petitions made on behalf of
these Christians. Paul had previously written of the immeasurable
riches of God in 1:7 and 2:7; here he prayed that *according to the
riches of his glory,* God would grant his requests. Because the

riches of God's glory are without measure, Paul prayed that the answers would be given to believers without measure and beyond their comprehension.

Paul first prayed that God would grant strength to these believers. The Greek word for "strength" is the opposite of "discouraged" in 3:13. We find the source of this strength in the Holy Spirit. The *inner being* refers to the deep center of the personality. Christians have a regenerated inner being that can be renewed and *strengthened* day by day *with power through his Spirit.* Paul wrote to the Corinthians, "So we do not lose heart. Even though our outer nature is wasting away, our inner nature is being renewed day by day" (2 Corinthians 4:16 NRSV). Paul prayed that the believers' inner beings would be strengthened.

God sent the Holy Spirit to be with and within his followers after Christ had returned to heaven. The Spirit would comfort them, guide them to know his truth, remind them of Jesus' words, point out when they did not obey, give them the right words to say, and fill them with power to do good (John 14–16). After Pentecost (Acts 2:1-4), God made the Holy Spirit available to all who believed in Jesus. We receive the Holy Spirit when we believe in Jesus Christ as Savior.

The Spirit provides power for our new lives. He begins a life-long process to make us more like Christ (2 Corinthians 3:17-18). When we receive Christ by faith, we begin an immediate personal relationship with God. The Holy Spirit works in us to help us become like Christ. He aids in prayer (Romans 8:26-27; Ephesians 2:18; 6:18); he inspires us to worship (Ephesians 5:18; Philippians 3:3); he shapes our character (Galatians 5:22-23). Furthermore, the Spirit unites the Christian community in Christ (Ephesians 2:19-22). The Spirit can be experienced by all, and he works through all (1 Corinthians 12:11; Ephesians 4:4). As such, the Spirit constantly provides us with the moral power to stand for Christ and to serve him. We access this power through prayer and through worship.

PRAYER POWER

How do we get strength to live morally, to be a witness, and to remain unified with other believers? We get strength from the powerful Holy Spirit. This power raised Christ from the dead (1:19-20). This power energized Paul's ministry (3:7). This power helps us defeat Satan in battle (6:10-11). How do we gain access to this power? We gain power in prayer. If you want power to live, make prayer a greater priority. When you pray, you will experience God's renovating power.

3:17-18 So that Christ may dwell in your hearts through faith.[NIV] The
Greek word translated *dwell* conveys the idea of settling down,
taking up permanent residence. Christ finds his home in believers'
hearts. The "heart" in the Bible always refers to the center of a
person's emotions and will. Christ takes up permanent residence,
changing a person's "heart" and, consequently, his or her words and
thoughts. "Through faith" refers to believers' faith. Christ takes up
residence in the hearts of those who through faith accept him as
their Savior and Lord.

**And I pray that you, being rooted and established in love,
may have power, together with all the saints, to grasp how
wide and long and high and deep is the love of Christ.**[NIV]
Christ's indwelling presence and the Spirit's strengthening
power also help believers to be *rooted and established in love*
(literally "having been rooted and having been founded,"
emphasizing the present result of a past action). In Greek, this
clause connects with 3:18 (as above), suggesting that by being
"rooted" we will then be able to understand the magnitude of
God's love. "Rooted" brings to mind the stable image of trees.
"Established" (also translated "grounded") brings to mind the
solid foundation of a building.

Paul prayed that this foundation of
love would give all believers *power . . .
to grasp* the vastness of Christ's love.
"Grasp" indicates reaching out for a
goal and holding onto it. We reach out
to attain this understanding *together
with all the saints.* No single believer

> We are never nearer
> Christ than when we
> find ourselves lost in a
> holy amazement at his
> unspeakable love.
>
> *John Owen*

can assimilate the mystery (3:9), the wisdom (3:10), or the riches
(3:6, 8) by himself or herself; it takes all the believers.

Christ's love is total, complete, eternal, and all-encompassing.
It reaches every corner of our experience. This passage shows that
even as we seek to grasp an understanding of Christ's love, we will
never understand it completely, for it is beyond our comprehension.
It is *wide*—covering the breadth of our own experience and reaching out to the whole world. It is *long*—continuing the length of our
lives and on into eternity. It is *high*—rising to the heights of our
celebration and elation. His love is *deep*—reaching to the depths
of discouragement, despair, and even death. Various attempts have
been made to identify the four dimensions—wide, long, high, and
deep—with the four arms of the cross, the four dimensions of the
heavenly city (Revelation 21:16), or the four dimensions of the
universe. Most likely, they should all be taken together as referring
to the all-encompassing majesty of the love of God.

HOW BIG?
How big is the love of Christ? how wide? how long? how high? how deep? Paul prays that we will know. We may never fully grasp the measure of Christ's love for us, but these verses give a hint as to the dimensions. It is as wide as the outstretched arms of the crucified Savior, embracing Jew and Gentile, rich and poor, male and female . . . reaching out to "whosoever will." It reaches low enough to touch the most wretched sinners and high enough to reconcile them to a holy God. The love of Christ is big enough to have room for the divorced and the never married . . . the sexually abused and the abuser . . . the woman who's had an abortion and the man who caused her to do it . . . the person addicted to alcohol or to pornography. How big is his love? As big as the cross.

3:19 **To know the love of Christ which passes knowledge; that you may be filled with all the fullness of God.**NKJV "To know the love of Christ" continues the thought from 3:18, which also speaks of the love of Christ. Paul prayed in 3:18 that the believers might "grasp" Christ's love. Here he prayed that they might "know" it (or experience it). Paul also recognized that Christ's love *passes knowledge.* He wanted the believers to know something that is beyond knowing. This is not a contradiction but a literary method to stress the same fact as in 3:18, that Christ's love is unfathomable. Believers cannot rationally explain Christ's love; they can only know it by experiencing it. This knowledge requires a continuous growing experience.

> I know of no truth in the whole Bible that ought to come home to us with such power and tenderness as that of the love of God. *D. L. Moody*

As believers get to know Christ better, they will *be filled with all the fullness of God.* This "fullness" means that there is nothing lacking in our relationship to the Father. God pours his love and power into believers, making us complete for this life and readying us for the life to come. "The fullness of God" is fully expressed only in Christ (Colossians 2:9-10). We need not look anywhere else. But we must appropriate his presence and power through faith and through prayer as we daily live for him. The ultimate goal is for believers to become Christlike individuals, filled so totally with Christ that he is seen in us. Paul's prayer for the Ephesians is also for you. You can ask the Holy Spirit to fill every aspect of your life to the fullest. (See also 1:23 and commentary there.)

3:20 **Now to Him who is able to do exceedingly abundantly above all that we ask or think, according to the power that works**

in us.NKJV Our thoughts include more than we dare to ask in our prayers; our dreams exceed what we consciously desire. God answers prayer; he even answers unspoken prayers. God can act beyond our ability to ask or even imagine. Paul uses three superlatives to drive home his point: God is able to do *exceedingly abundantly above* anything we would dare to ask, think, or imagine. God is far above and beyond our finite minds. God "is able" because of his awesome *power.* To the unfathomable depths of Christ's love is added the exceeding abundance of his power. Believers can claim Christ's great love (3:19) and know that his power *works in* us through the Holy Spirit. See Romans 16:25 and Jude 24 for two other doxologies that praise God for his power.

ABUNDANTLY ABOVE
As Paul wrote these words, he was under house arrest in Rome. Christianity at that time was considered a small, troublesome sect of Judaism. Believers were persecuted and often exiled. How, then, could Paul write, "To Him who is able to do exceedingly abundantly above all that we ask or think"? He could write it because he had personally experienced the power of God in his own life—a power that would rapidly outgrow and outlast the mighty Roman Empire; that would cause the gospel to spread throughout Europe, transforming it; that would inspire such thinkers and leaders as Augustine, Aquinas, Luther, and Calvin; that would launch the Protestant Reformation and eventually lead to the building of the "New World," a world where religious freedom and tolerance would rise to unparalleled heights. That is "the power that works in us."

3:21 To Him be glory in the church by Christ Jesus to all generations, forever and ever. Amen.NKJV God alone deserves *glory,* for he alone is glorious. The word "glory" refers to the wonderful and awe-inspiring but indescribable presence of God himself. Glory is given to God *in the church.* The church, God's creation, exists to glorify him. The church is the sphere of the outworking of God's plan here on earth (3:10). The ability to give glory to God comes only *by Christ Jesus,* for he brought the church into existence through his sacrifice for sin and his resurrection from the dead. This glory will be made known *to all generations, forever and ever.*

This doxology—prayer of praise to God—ends part 1 of Ephesians. Some have thought that this doxology was originally the end of this letter. More likely, Paul simply broke into spontaneous words of praise growing out of his prayer (3:14-19).

In the first section, Paul described the timeless role of the church. In part 2 (chapters 4–6), he explained how church members should live in order to bring about the unity God wants. As in most of his books, Paul first laid a doctrinal foundation and then followed with practical applications of the truths he presented.

Ephesians 4:1–5:5

WE ARE ONE BODY IN CHRIST / 4:1-16

Here the focus changes from theological to practical. Paul has explained to his readers God's great mystery and plan for his church, and he has prayed an awe-inspiring prayer that they might know all of Christ's love and all of his blessings. The remainder of the letter contains Paul's plea to live out the grace and unity the believers had received through Christ. Verses 1-6 are on unity; verses 7-16 are on diversity in the church. The challenges for churches today parallel the challenges that faced first-century churches like the one in Ephesus. We must remain unified as believers, incorporating our diversity so that we can serve and glorify our Lord.

4:1 Therefore I, a prisoner for serving the Lord, beg you to lead a life worthy of your calling, for you have been called by God.NLT The word "therefore" connects this sentence to Paul's words in the previous chapters—the great mystery God has revealed to us in his church. Paul was imprisoned in Rome *for serving the Lord* (that is, his imprisonment was a result of his preaching the gospel, see Acts 21:27–22:22). Despite the chains that bound him physically and kept him from traveling, Paul continued to write, in this case urging the Ephesian believers to *lead a life worthy of your calling* and to remember that they had been *called by God* (1:4). Their "call" to salvation was accomplished through Christ's humble act of dying on the cross for our sin. It was also a "call" to service for God.

CALLED
God has chosen us to be Christ's representatives on earth. In light of this truth, we should live worthy of the calling we have received—the privilege of being selected as Christ's very own. This includes being humble, gentle, patient, understanding, and peaceful. People are watching your life. Can they see Christ in you? How well are you doing as his representative?

How can one live *worthy* of the calling? The Greek word for "worthy" *(axios)* refers to a balance, as on scales. Thus, believers are to live "in balance" with their calling. How they act should match what they believe. Remembering Christ's sacrifice should cause believers to live for his glory in every area of their lives. The following verses describe how to do this.

4:2 Be completely humble and gentle.[NIV] This verse lists four characteristics of a person who is "worthy of the calling." Believers make up the church, the body of Christ. Thus, believers, by privilege of their responsibility, must be together, serve together, and worship together. The following characteristics help create and maintain smooth relationships among people.

Both the Greek and Roman cultures considered humility and gentleness to be weak character traits showing a lack of self-respect. The Old Testament, however, paved the way for a positive connotation for humility because God "lives with" the humble: "For this is what the high and lofty One says—he who lives forever, whose name is holy: 'I live in a high and holy place, but also with him who is contrite and lowly in spirit, to revive the spirit of the lowly and to revive the heart of the contrite'" (Isaiah 57:15 NIV). Jesus exalted humility as a virtue when he said, "You call me 'Teacher' and 'Lord,' and rightly so, for that is what I am. Now that I, your Lord and Teacher, have washed your feet, you also should wash one another's feet. I have set you an example that you should do as I have done for you" (John 13:13-15 NIV). Christ expected his followers to be humble not only before God but toward one another— serving one another and not putting themselves "above" anyone else. Christ is our example; thus, we must also *be completely humble.*

> He who cannot forgive others breaks the bridge over which he must pass himself.
>
> *George Herbert*

Believers are also to be *gentle.* Humility is an attitude, and gentleness is the action derived from it. Gentle people do not attempt to grab for positions of importance or assert authority over others. Gentle people accept God's dealings with them without arguing or resisting. Gentle people are considerate of others. If everyone in a church had the characteristics of humility and gentleness, conflicts would disappear and members would have strength and power in their service.

Be patient, bearing with one another in love.[NIV] Patience (also translated "long-suffering") conveys the quality of being able to handle one another's faults and failures and refusing to avenge wrongs. No one is ever going to be perfect here on earth, so believers must *be patient* with one another despite their faults. *Bearing with one another in love* is the action side of patience. Very similar in meaning to "patience," "bearing with one another" emphasizes the willingness to forgive and involves empathizing with the other person. To show patience requires *love,* which ought to be the guiding principle for all of a believer's actions, even when natural differences and clashes occur. Bearing with one another presupposes that, at times, loving others will be a burden. Believers must be willing to carry the load without expecting reward, thanks, or return.

WHAT A VIRTUE!
Perhaps no other virtue seems so foreign to our culture as patience. Be honest: Do you ever stand by the microwave, tapping your foot impatiently as you wait for it to heat something? practically pull the paper out of the fax machine because it is working too slowly? swerve between lanes on the highway in order to get ahead a few car lengths? If these aren't your particular problem areas, do you struggle with impatience in other areas? If you answered no to all the above, give yourself an *F,* for lying. We live in an instant world, and we expect instant results and instant gratification. Yet Paul instructs us to be patient with one another. How? We can start by reflecting on the patience God shows toward us—boundless, unmerited, compassionate—and then letting that same grace flow through us to others.

4:3 Endeavoring to keep the unity of the Spirit in the bond of peace.[NKJV] True *unity* among believers follows naturally from the characteristics described in 4:2 and provides the theme for verses 3-6. Such unity is only possible when the Holy Spirit acts in believers' lives—the Spirit originates and sustains oneness among believers. Love for each other, which the presence of the Spirit causes, makes peace possible. The *bond of peace* includes the idea of uniting the members into one body. This "bond" holds people together, like string or twine. Peace functions as the "binding twine" of unity. God gives it to us, producing equality and understanding.

The Holy Spirit builds unity. He leads, but we have to be willing to be led and to do our part to keep the peace. The word "endeavoring" points to our part in the process (see also 1 Thessalonians

> We cannot expect the world to believe that the Father sent the Son, that Jesus' claims are true and that Christianity is true, unless the world sees some reality of the oneness of true Christians.
> *Francis Schaeffer*

2:17; 2 Timothy 2:15; 2 Peter 1:10, 15; 3:14). Believers cannot experience unity without the presence of the Holy Spirit, and neither can they maintain unity without allowing the Spirit to work in their lives. The Greek word translated endeavoring or "make every effort" is *spoudazontes.* The Greek word has no sense of the possibility of failure ("just try, even though you might fail"). The word conveys the idea of working toward something difficult with a determination to make it happen. Paul knew that maintaining unity among believers would take hard work and continual diligence. Believers face many attempts to tear apart their unity. False teachers would arise, even from within their ranks, attempting to divide the people; persecution would attempt to frighten the church and send it scattering. The believers in each of the churches in and around Ephesus would need to work diligently to maintain their unity. Churches today need the same quality of diligence in maintaining *the unity of the Spirit in the bond of peace.*

UNITY
There are an infinite number of issues that divide us—doctrinal beliefs, worship style, race, language—and only one force that will keep us together: "endeavoring to keep the unity of the Spirit in the bond of peace." Unity can come only through the Spirit; it will remain only if we are diligent to maintain it. Unity is like a fire—it tends to die out if unattended. Would an objective observer describe your attitudes and actions as unifying or divisive? We have a clear command from Scripture: Work diligently to preserve unity.

4:4 There is one body and one Spirit.^{NRSV} Why should believers diligently maintain their unity (as described in 4:3)? Paul answered that question here. The words "there is" could be translated "because there is," connecting these verses with the previous verses that describe the bonds of unity. We must work to maintain our unity because Christ desires it—there is only *one body and one Spirit.* The repetition of the word "one" in verses 4-6 emphasizes this unity. Regardless of all that can divide the believers—racial background, social status, and gender, to name a few—Christians belong to one body, through one Holy Spirit (see also 1:13-14; 2:11-22; 3:6). In a pagan culture, people can choose from any number of cults to join and gods to worship. For Christians, however, there is only one body, unified by one Spirit.

The unity in the body of believers occurs because one Spirit indwells them. The Holy Spirit lives in all Christians and gives to the church its true oneness (2:18). Without the Spirit, the body could not exist. Christianity is not a club to join, nor is it some mystical but unreal entity. Instead, true Christianity is a spiritual relationship with Christ as well as with other believers. Through the Spirit, all believers are united in one universal body. Christ's true body (all Christians from all ages) is already united under one Head (Christ), but that unity is not yet fully realized. After Christ returns, the unity of his church will be fully visible.

> Satan separates; God unites; love binds us together.   *D. L. Moody*

Verses 4-6 explain the unity of the believers, relating to the unity in the Trinity (the Spirit in 4:4, the Son in 4:5, and the Father in 4:6).

Just as you were called to the one hope of your calling.^{NRSV} The "one Spirit" is the "deposit guaranteeing our inheritance" (1:14). That inheritance includes "the hope to which he has called" us (1:18). All believers *were called to the one hope* of our calling—that is, to eternal life in God's kingdom. Because the one Spirit made us part of one body, we are all promised "one hope." Jewish and Gentile believers have a common privilege, a common calling, and a common hope. Unlike the modern use of the word "hope" ("I sure hope this happens, but I don't know if it will"), Christian hope is an expectation of full salvation ("I expect the Lord's return").

SICK OR HEALTHY?
Muscular dystrophy is a terrible disease. The person with MD has all the right parts and equipment available—brain cells, neurons, axons, dendrites, muscles—but they don't work properly. The problem is not in the brain. The brain sends the appropriate signals. The problem lies between the nerve and the muscle. The nerve conveys the brain's message, such as move, turn, lift, etc., but the muscle does not respond. The body is essentially nonresponsive to the brain's commands. Ephesians 4:4-6 states that there is one body and one Lord over the body—Jesus. What happens when we don't obey his commands, follow his lead? We have a sick body. How healthy a part of the body are you? Promote well-being in the church by being a responsive servant. Don't do anything that tears it down.

4:5 One Lord, one faith, one baptism.^{NRSV} This verse focuses on Christ. "One Lord" refers to Jesus Christ, whose lordship (headship) forms the basis of unity in the body. Christians worship one Lord. There are not many real gods from which to choose; there is only one—the Lord Jesus Christ. Wherever people believe in Jesus Christ alone and trust in his death and resurrection for their salvation, they are joined with all other believers because of this *one faith.* This faith alone saves; this faith is the one and only "way" (John 14:6). This one faith binds all believers together.

The act of believing is manifested through the act of baptism, the symbol of being brought into the body. (Faith and baptism are similarly connected in Mark 16:16 and Colossians 2:12.) Paul's inclusion of this *one baptism* reveals the great importance that baptism held for the early church. Baptism replaced circumcision as the initiation rite of the new order, the new covenant. "Baptism" refers here to baptism in water, as opposed to baptism by the Spirit, because of the word's placement in this verse. If Paul had meant the baptism of the Holy Spirit, he would have placed it in the previous verse. Christians need only "one baptism" by which they publicly acknowledge their one faith in one Lord. Paul wrote in 1 Corinthians 12:13, "For in the one Spirit we were all baptized into one body—Jews or Greeks, slaves or free—and we were all made to drink of one Spirit" (NRSV). This expression of faith through baptism brings unity to believers.

ONE
The sounds of Gregorian chants echoing in a European monastery chapel . . . shouts of "Aleluya!" and "Sí, Señor Jesucristo!" in a house church in Mexico . . . the rich, layered harmonies of gospel music from an African chorus . . . quiet, fervent prayers uttered in a stained-glass worship center in America . . . What do these strikingly different kinds of worship expression have in common? "There is one body and one Spirit, . . . one Lord, one faith, one baptism; one God and Father of all." We, the body of Christ, come in all the colors of the rainbow and with as many different ways to worship him. Rather than let those things act as barriers between us, why not celebrate our diversity, our different-ness? We are different, but we are one body in Christ.

4:6 One God and Father of all, who is above all and through all and in all.NRSV This verse focuses on God the Father. There are not many gods, as in the pagan culture; there is only *one God.* As the only God, he alone deserves our worship and praise. *Father of all* means that he is the Creator. All people were made in his image (Genesis 1:26). The sovereign God completely controls his creation. Christians understand themselves as God's creation and as God's "called." God *is above all*—supreme, transcendent, the

THE ONENESS OF ALL BELIEVERS

Too often believers are separated because of minor differences in doctrine. But this passage shows those areas where Christians must agree to attain true unity. When believers have this unity of spirit, petty differences should never be allowed to dissolve that unity.

Believers are one in:	*Our unity is experienced in:*
Body	The fellowship of believers—the church
Spirit	The Holy Spirit, who activates the fellowship
Hope	That glorious future to which we are all called
Lord	Christ, to whom we all belong
Faith	Our singular commitment to Christ
Baptism	Baptism—the sign of entry into the church
God	God, who is our Father

ruler over all of his creation. God is *through all*—actively present and pervasive in every part of his creation. God is *in all*—he himself lives within his people. Any view of God that violates either his transcendence, pervasiveness, or immanence does not paint a true picture of God. Paul did not teach pantheism ("God is in everything, so we can worship nature") or universalism ("God is Father of all and will therefore save everyone"). Rather, he taught about the omnipotent, omnipresent, and omniscient God, ruling over creation and exercising his power through his followers on behalf of the church.

4:7 But to each one of us grace has been given as Christ apportioned it.[NIV] Although the church is one unified body, each of its members has a special ability to be used for the good and growth of all. No one is overlooked; everyone is important to building up the community. The word "grace" is used here as it was in 3:2, 7-8, referring to the privilege of having been called by God. Although Christians are called to be unified, God in his wisdom did not make believers photocopies of one another. Instead, each believer is given grace (one or more gifts) *as Christ apportioned it.* In his infinite wisdom, Christ gave different gifts to different people. Every believer has a gift; no one has

> The church of Christ needs servants of all kinds, and instruments of every sort; penknives as well as swords, axes as well as hammers, chisels as well as saws, Marthas as well as Marys, Peters as well as Johns.
>
> *J. C. Ryle*

all the gifts. In this way, believers need one another in the church as they seek to accomplish the work of the kingdom.

BOXED GIFTS
One hundred trained, talented musicians playing together can produce music that is breathtakingly beautiful. The same one hundred musicians playing independently of each other can produce earsplitting noise. The difference is that while the second group is completely self-absorbed, focusing only on themselves, the first group is in harmony, concentrating on the music and following the conductor. The analogy for the church should be obvious. When we focus on following the Lord and fulfilling his purposes for us, it is a beautiful—even awesome—thing to see. When we focus on ourselves and pursue our own selfish agendas, it is a pitiful or even laughable sight. God has given to each believer gifts according to Christ's own matchless gift. These gifts are not just for our own personal benefit, however; they are for the good of the whole body. What are you doing with yours?

4:8 Therefore it is said, "When he ascended on high he made captivity itself a captive; he gave gifts to his people."[NRSV] The phrase "therefore it is said" is a favorite rabbinic introduction to a scriptural quotation. It conveys and reaffirms the divine authority of Scripture. Here it introduces a scriptural basis for spiritual gifts. Psalm 68:18 pictures God as conqueror as the ark of the covenant was being brought up to Zion in triumph by David (2 Samuel 6; 1 Chronicles 15). It had been removed in battle. As David returns the ark to Jerusalem, he also brings the tribute of war extracted from the captured foes. Some of the spoils was given to the temple, and some was distributed among the warriors. Paul used that picture to refer to Christ's ascent into heaven. The work and authority for apportioning spiritual gifts rightly belongs to the ascended Christ. Paul's development of this theme prepares readers for his thoughts in 4:11. In the psalm, the victory is over David's foes. In Paul's reference, Christ, the Son of David, is triumphant in destroying his foe Satan. In the psalm, the conqueror receives gifts and, as was the custom, distributes a portion of the spoils to his people. Paul's reference means that God began to give special gifts to people following Christ's return to heaven.

The statement "he made captivity itself a captive" has one of two meanings: (1) He led the captured ones (as one would lead a train of vanquished foes) into their captivity, or (2) he captured the captors (that is, he reversed the captivity; he enslaved the enslavers). Both meanings imply that Christ vanquished our

enemies (such as death, Satan, and sin) and captivated them. He
returned in triumph to heaven *(ascended on high)* and, in turn,
gave gifts to his people.

Paul seemed to have reversed the meaning of Psalm 68:18,
which says of God, "You received gifts from men." Paul quoted
a Scripture that reads, "He gave gifts to his people." Was Paul
misquoting? Several explanations have been given. Two appear
most plausible. One approach argues that Paul was functioning
as a prophet and revealing God's intended meaning by changing
the words, and that he was supplying the concrete meaning
implied in the Old Testament setting and applying it to Christ.
When a king receives tribute, he does so in order to then give it
to his troops and replenish his treasuries. This could be what God
instructed Paul to say in this verse. A second explanation is more
likely, however. It was common for rabbis to quote translations
of Old Testament passages that best reinforced their arguments.
Paul probably used an ancient Targum (an Aramaic translation of
the Hebrew text) to make his point. In the Targum, the word is
actually changed from "received" to "gave."

Paul used the picture from this psalm to explain how Christ
conquered his enemies, returned to glory, and bestowed gifts
on his church. The gifts God gave to his church (in the form of
people called to special functions) are described in 4:11-12.

**4:9-10 (What does "he ascended" mean except that he also descended
to the lower, earthly regions? He who descended is the very one
who ascended higher than all the heavens, in order to fill the
whole universe.)**[NIV] Paul reasoned that Christ's ascent implies a
previous descent. The phrase "lower, earthly regions" represents
the farthest extreme from the heights of heaven. Paul may have
been thinking of Christ's descent into hell and freeing the captives
there (see Acts 2:27-28; see Life Application Bible commentary
on 1 Peter 3:18-22 for a lengthy discussion). More likely, these
"lower regions" refer to the earth, the place where the Son came
in his incarnation. The "captives" (4:8) then would be either Satan
and his hosts or the saints who were taken "captive" or "called"
(a reference to election).

The same Christ *who descended is the very one who ascended.*
As a result of his descent and ascent, nothing is hidden from him.
All things are subject to him; no realm in heaven or earth is
beyond his control. That he "ascended" means not that he left
the earth and involvement in it but rather that he completely fills
all things. That Christ will *fill the whole universe* refers to his
power and control over all of his creation. Christ is Lord of the
whole universe—past, present, and future. He fills all things with

himself as their sovereign Head, yet he fills the church, his body, with the blessings of his Spirit, grace, and gifts (see also 1:10, 23).

OPEN YOUR GIFT
Oneness in Christ does not destroy individuality. The Holy Spirit has given each Christian special gifts for building up the church. Now that we have these gifts, it is crucial to use them. Are you spiritually mature, exercising the gifts God has given you? If you know what your gifts are, look for opportunities to serve. If you don't know, ask God to show you, perhaps with the help of your minister or Christian friends. Then, as you begin to recognize your special area of service, use your gifts to strengthen and encourage the church.

4:11 The gifts he gave were that some would be apostles, some prophets, some evangelists, some pastors and teachers.^{NRSV} This expands on the thought begun in 4:7-8 regarding the gifts Christ *gave*. In this context, these gifts are actually people who have been called to special functions. Not all people have all the gifts, for Paul was clear to explain that *some* would be gifted in one area and *some* in another. The list given here is by no means complete (for other types of gifts, see Romans 12; 1 Corinthians 12). According to the Greek, all the people listed are direct objects of "gave," indicating that God gave these people to the church as gifts. The offices listed here focus mainly on those who proclaim the gospel and teach the truth.

First listed are the *apostles* and *prophets,* about whom we have already read. They are the foundation for Christ's temple (see 2:20 and 3:6 and commentary there). "Apostles" included the eleven men Jesus called (without Judas), plus others who are called apostles—such as Paul himself (Romans 1:1), Matthias (Acts 1:26), Barnabas (Acts 14:14), Jesus' brother James (Galatians 1:19), Silas (1 Thessalonians 2:6), Andronicus and Junias (Romans 16:7). It seems that the qualifications for being an apostle were to have seen the risen Christ, to have been sent out by him to preach the gospel, and to be working on behalf of the kingdom, building its foundation (as noted in 2:20). Paul also notes "signs, wonders, and miracles" as marks of a true apostle (2 Corinthians 12:12).

God also gave *prophets* to the church. These people, also laborers on the church's "foundation" (2:20), had special gifts in ministering God's messages to his people. At times they would foretell the future (Acts 11:28; 21:9, 11), but more often their job was to exhort, encourage, and strengthen God's people (Acts 15:32;

1 Corinthians 14:29). God spoke through prophets—inspiring them with specific messages for particular times and places.

The *evangelists* were the traveling ministers, similar to the missionaries of today. They went to non-Christian people and proclaimed the gospel to them, often being the first to start a church in a particular area (Acts 21:8; 2 Timothy 4:5).

Next, God gave *pastors and teachers.* These two gifts are likely the same. While the apostles, prophets, and evangelists had a universal sphere of function (the church as a whole), the pastors and teachers probably served in the local churches. Like shepherds, they tended God's "flock," handling the day-to-day affairs of their congregation—administering, counseling, guiding, feeding.

WHO'S YOUR MINISTER?
How many ministers are there in your church? One? Three? If it's a big church—eight or ten? Before you answer that question, read Ephesians 4:11-12 carefully. Here Paul shows that God gives pastors and teachers to his church not to *be* the ministers of the church but to *equip* the ministers. Who then are the ministers? All Christians are to be ministers, so you are one of them. The role of pastors and teachers is to train and equip the "saints" (all believers) to be able to serve in whatever ways that God has called them. So if your church has one hundred members and only one minister, there's a big problem. We are all called to be ministers. What is your ministry? How are you being equipped for it? In what ways are you using that training and your gift(s) for the building up of the body?

4:12 To equip the saints for the work of ministry, for building up the body of Christ.NRSV These specially gifted people (4:11) were given to the church for one ultimate goal: *to equip the saints.* The word for "equip" means to make right, like the setting of a broken bone, or to bring to completion by training or restoring. The apostles, prophets, evangelists, pastors, and teachers furnish and equip the believers to do the work of the ministry, which results in the *building up the body of Christ.* The church builds itself in the faith as the members care for one another, show love, and generally manifest the other gifts God gives (as mentioned in Romans 12 and 1 Corinthians 12). Yet the church also builds itself as it reaches out to its surrounding community with the love of Christ, drawing others into the fold. God has given his church an enormous responsibility—to make disciples in every nation (Matthew 28:18-20). This involves preaching, teaching, healing, nurturing, giving, administering, building, and many other tasks. Fulfilling this command solo would be impossible. But God calls us as members of his body. No one should be a bystander, an observer. Everyone must do *the work of ministry.* Some of us can do one task; some can do another. Together we can obey God more fully than any of us could alone. We tend to overestimate what we can do by ourselves and underestimate what we can do as a group. But as the body of Christ, we can accomplish more together than we could dream possible working by ourselves. Working together, the church can express the fullness of Christ.

4:13 Until we come to such unity in our faith and knowledge of God's Son that we will be mature and full grown in the Lord, measuring up to the full stature of Christ.[NLT] The word "until" indicates that the process described in 4:12 must continue until a certain end is achieved—when all believers *come to* (arrive at, attain) unity (see Philippians 3:11). While unity of the Spirit must be maintained (4:3), *unity in our faith* must be attained. The "unity of faith" means a unity of belief in Christ himself, and this belief relates intrinsically to our knowledge of him. The goal includes making a united effort to live out and proclaim this faith.

Unity in our *knowledge* refers to fuller and more complete experiential knowledge. Every believer must have a personal, intimate relationship with Jesus Christ. Paul here called him *God's Son,* showing that this knowledge includes an appropriate understanding of the new relationship with the Father that has been provided by the Son (Romans 8:10-17).

This unified body of believers is called to *be mature and full grown, measuring up to the full stature of Christ.* The focus is on "we" in this verse—every believer as part of the entire body. This metaphor means that the church, as Christ's body, must match the Head in growth and maturity. This does not speak of perfection (impossible in this life) but of growth—such as children growing into adults, which ties into the following advice regarding this growth. (See Luke 2:52, where Jesus grew "in stature.")

4:14 We must no longer be children, tossed to and fro and blown about by every wind of doctrine, by people's trickery, by their craftiness in deceitful scheming.[NRSV] Because believers are called to maturity in the faith (4:13), they *must no longer be children* (or like helpless infants). Christ requires childlike faith (referring to trust and acceptance—Matthew 19:14). This, however, pictures children who are easily led astray. Believers should avoid this error. People who are "children" in their faith and knowledge must grow up and mature (4:13). Otherwise, they are susceptible to false teaching *(every wind of doctrine).* They will be unstable, rootless, without direction, and susceptible to manipulation. A small boat on a lake, *tossed to and fro and blown about,* is unable to stay on a course and reach its destination. Immature believers, like children, are unable to discern *trickery* and *craftiness* and thus will be knocked about with various teachings contrary to God's Word. False teachers work like cheating gamblers, who load the dice in order to trick people. Uncritical acceptance of new teachings will keep their minds in as much turmoil as a stormy sea. Indeed, false teaching was a major problem in the early church (see, for example, Galatians 1:6-9; 3:1-14; Colossians 2:6-23). Believers must be growing toward maturity in true faith. Only then will they be able to discern false doctrines; only then will they stay the course and reach the goal of maturity (4:13).

STANDING FIRM
Paul often warned the churches against false teachers. In fact, the central theme of the letter to the Colossians dealt with false teaching. As believers, we must be aware (but not unduly suspicious) of every issue as heresy. We must very carefully sort out essential from nonessential issues. In Ephesians, the problem wasn't so much outright *heresy* as it was *assimilation.* Assimilation meant that the false teachers were including Paul's teaching in what they taught, thus diluting the truth. They combined lots of religious and philosophical thoughts and undermined the central authority of Christ's gospel.

The Ephesian church had a history of being plagued with heresy. Around A.D. 58, Paul first warned the Ephesian elders of subtle heresies creeping into their congregation (see Acts 20:26-31). According to Ephesians (written in A.D. 61), he warned them again about false teaching, and then he made stronger censures in his epistles to Timothy (written in A.D. 64 and 66), who was working in Ephesus (see 1 Timothy 1:3-6; 4:1-2; 6:20-21; 2 Timothy 1:13-14; 2:14-26). If 1 John was also addressed to the Ephesian church (and many scholars think it was), the church was still fighting with heretics in the 80s (see 1 John 2:18-19; 4:1-3). And even in the 90s, when Revelation was written, the Ephesian church was still testing false apostles (see Revelation 2:1-7).

Beware of teachers or philosophies that say, "We're both saying the same thing," or "These key ideas like salvation and redemption are the same in all religions." New Age philosophies and comparative religion classes find patterns of similarity in all faiths. While some parallels exist, they do not explain away the basis for faith. Jesus said, "Whoever believes in the Son has eternal life" (John 3:36 NRSV), not "Let each person find God in his own way." Jesus said, "Whoever drinks the water I give him will never thirst" (John 4:14 NIV), not "Whatever drink you choose will be as good as any other." When faced with challenges to our faith, Christians must seek help and study the issues so as to stand firm against false teaching.

4:15 But speaking the truth in love, we must grow up in every way into him who is the head, into Christ.[NRSV] Believers are not to be like immature children (4:14). In their witness for Christ, they need not resort to trickery and scheming as do the false teachers (4:14). Instead, their continuous objective should be to *grow up in every way into him who is the head, into Christ,* measuring up to his full stature, as described in 4:13.

Believers should want to be like Christ, the truth (John 14:6), and be strengthened by the Holy Spirit, who guides the church, the Spirit of truth (John 16:13). Satan, by contrast, is the father of lies (John 8:44). As followers of Christ, we must be committed to the truth. This means that our words should be honest

> Truth becomes hard if not softened by love; love becomes soft if it is not strengthened by truth. The apostle calls us to hold the two together.
> *John R. W. Stott*

and that our actions should reflect Christ's integrity. Speaking the truth in love is not always easy, convenient, or pleasant, but it is necessary if the church is going to do Christ's work in the world.

How can believers "grow up into Christ"? The answer is that Christ forms us into a body—a group of individuals who are united in their purpose and in their love for one another and for the Lord. If one person stumbles, the rest of the group can pick that person up and help him or her walk with God again. If an individual sins, he or she can find restoration through the church (Galatians 6:1), even as the rest of the body continues to witness to God's truth. As part of Christ's body, do you reflect part of Christ's character and carry out your special role in his work?

SPEAK . . . IN LOVE
In describing the mature Christian, Paul says that one of the marks is "speaking the truth in love." This sounds so simple, but it seems so hard for us to do. Some of us are fairly good at speaking the truth, but we forget to be loving. We call ourselves "prophets"; others call us jerks or something less flattering. Some of us are good at being loving, but we don't have it in us to level with others if the truth is painful. We call ourselves "Christlike"; others call us wimps. Or worse. The instruction here is to do both: Speak the truth, but do it in a loving manner. Think of the trouble we would spare ourselves if we followed this practice, especially in the church! When you have a problem with another believer, don't go to someone else with it. Go directly to that person, and speak the truth in love.

4:16 From him the whole body, joined and held together by every supporting ligament, grows and builds itself up in love, as each

SPIRITUAL GIFTS

What does the Bible say about the nature and use of spiritual gifts?

Read Romans 12; Ephesians 4.	God gives us spiritual gifts so that we can work together to serve him and each other. God gives us gifts so that we can build up his church. Our gifts, though different, are all useful. Christians, using their gifts to serve God and each other, create an exciting fellowship.
Read 1 Corinthians 12; 1 Peter 4:10-11.	Spiritual gifts have a single source and a special purpose. Spiritual gifts have at times been divisive because of people's jealousy. Spiritual gifts ought to be humbly used in service of others.
Read 1 Thessalonians 5:12-28.	Spiritual maturity encourages the proper use of spiritual gifts.

part does its work.[NIV] Christ is head of this body of believers (4:15) and its source; without him there could be no body, no church. From him alone the body *grows and builds itself up in love.* The reference to growing and building refers not so much to increased size as to increased faith and spiritual strength. This increase can occur because Christ, as head, supplies all the needs of the body. The description of believers *joined and held together by every supporting ligament* describes the bond in Christ that holds the church together. The "ligaments" are the joints, the junctures, the contiguous links that join together the various limbs at the point of contact. The ligament provides the means of support, as a contact point between parts of the body and as a way to transfer strength and balance to each part. "Joined" means integrated, being fitly joined together, as a fastening joint in house construction or as a shoulder joint for the body. "Held together" means being united, being kept firm, as in reconciling those who have quarreled (Colossians 2:19).

Believers from different backgrounds, nations, and languages, who make up *the whole body,* are held together by a strong bond and have the goal of growing spiritually. This happens *as each part does its work.* Each part contributes or "works in measure." The measure comes from that which Christ gives as a spiritual gift (4:7) and as the measure of the stature of Christ (4:13). Members of the body receive exactly what they need and are responsible to use what they have for the good of the whole. We receive gifts not for our own prestige or acclaim but to help build up other believers in the church.

LIVING AS A NEW PERSON / 4:17–5:5

People should be able to see a difference between Christians and non-Christians because of the way Christians live. The section from 4:17-24 appeals to believers to leave behind the old life of sin because they are followers of Christ—which should result in a radical change in their behavior. This change is further detailed in the section from 4:25–5:2, which lists negative characteristics that have no place in the church and positive characteristics that will reflect Christ's character.

Living the Christian life is a process. Although we have a new nature, we don't automatically think all good thoughts and express all right attitudes. But if we keep listening to God, we will be changing all the time. We must trust God to change us on the inside—our character, values, attitudes, perspective, and motives.

4:17 So I tell you this, and insist on it in the Lord, that you must no longer live as the Gentiles do, in the futility of their thinking.[NIV] Believers are to be maturing in their faith and using their gifts to benefit the church (4:11-16); therefore, they have a privilege as well as a responsibility. Paul could not stress too much the significant responsibility given to believers as they live in a sinful world. *So,* he wrote, *I tell you . . . and insist.* The words "in the Lord" provide the basis for the authority of what Paul was about to write.

The believers in Ephesus *must no longer live as the Gentiles do.* Many of the believers to whom Paul was writing were Gentiles by racial background. Because Paul was writing to many Gentiles, why did he say not to live "as the Gentiles do"? Paul was stressing that the Ephesian believers must abandon what had been their former way of life, not living any longer as the other Gentiles around them who were pagans, not Christians (see 1 Corinthians 12:2). How did the Gentiles live? *In the futility of their thinking,* referring to the natural tendency of human beings to employ intellectual pride, rationalizations, and excuses (Romans 1:21). Their thinking was "futile" because their lives were being wasted on worthless objects (idols), untrue teachings, and immoral behavior. The results of this futile way of thinking are described in the following verses.

4:18 They are darkened in their understanding and separated from the life of God because of the ignorance that is in them due to the hardening of their hearts.[NIV] This describes the unfortunate state of the unbelievers surrounding this core of believers in the church. The believers could no longer live as they previously did, for their prior lifestyle had been completely opposite of what they were presently experiencing. The unbelievers

are darkened in their understanding, while the believers have
found the light of Christ and are given his wisdom. The unbelievers are *separated from the life of God,* while the believers have
been made one with him through Christ. The unbelievers are in
ignorance, while the believers have access to the full knowledge
of the truth. The unbelievers have refused to believe after *hardening . . . their hearts,* while the believers have welcomed Christ
into their hearts. A fully hardened person is unable to respond to
God (see Exodus 11:10; Mark 8:17-18; Romans 11:8; Hebrews
3:7-8).

TURN ON THE LIGHTS
Having described mature believers in 4:13-16, Paul followed with
a brief description of nonbelievers. The first characteristics are
"futility of their thinking" and "darkened in their understanding."
They have "darkened minds." Have you ever tried to share your
faith in Christ with nonbelieving friends, even very intelligent ones,
and they have looked at you as though you were from Mars?
Your friends aren't stupid; they have darkened, unregenerate
minds. Of course, you should continue to give them a reasoned
defense of your faith if they're interested, but the struggle is not
really a matter of explanation. It's more a need for "illumination"—
for God to "turn the lights on." Continue to be ready to give a
defense to everyone who asks you (1 Peter 3:15), but even more
urgently, pray that God will lift the darkness.
    The next characteristic of nonbelievers is that they have "har-
dened hearts." The problem is not only intellectual; it is *willful,* too.
That's why it's almost impossible to argue someone into the
kingdom of heaven. People don't often reject Christ on intellectual
grounds; they reject him (or ignore him) because they don't want
to surrender their wills to his. If you are presenting Christ and you
receive an objection to every statement or truth claim, step back
and ask: Is this really an intellectual problem? Or is it just that this
person does not want to submit to Christ? If it's truly intellectual,
try to answer the objection. If it's more willful, recognize that and
deal with it on the heart level. Pray that God will turn on the lights
and illumine the darkened, hardened heart.

**4:19 Having lost all sensitivity, they have given themselves over to
sensuality so as to indulge in every kind of impurity, with a
continual lust for more.**[NIV] These unbelievers have *lost all sensitivity,* or have no feeling about their degenerate condition. Such
people are beyond feeling either shame for their evil or hope for
anything better concerning their condition before God.

    The logical next step for people who have lost all conscience
is that they *have given themselves over to sensuality* (lewd
behavior, lowest morals possible), *indulge in every kind of*

impurity (they work toward moral decadence as if it were their occupation), and *lust for more* (also translated "greediness," extreme selfishness without regard for others).

While these terms seem strong, we must understand the culture that surrounded the believers in and around Ephesus. The temple to the goddess Artemis (the Roman name was Diana) stood in Ephesus. (See the Introduction under "Audience" for more on this temple.) Artemis was the goddess of fertility in women, animals, and nature. On occasion, human sacrifices were given to Artemis. She was believed to be a moon goddess who helped women in childbirth. She is portrayed as the many-breasted earth mother. Her temple had a hierarchy of religious personnel, including eunuch priests, young virgins, and prostitute priestesses. One month every year was devoted to ceremonies honoring Artemis. A carnival atmosphere that included concerts, feasts, athletic games, and plays created opportunities for immorality, drunkenness, and sensuality. To the Jews, worship at the temple of Artemis was extremely corrupt. Christians, as well, were not to take part in its practices.

IN THE DARK
How had these Gentiles gone wrong? Their hearts and minds were rebellious against God. After darkened minds and darkened hearts comes . . . *darkened behavior.* Of course, what else would unregenerate hearts and minds generate? Like our own world, the Roman culture that formed the backdrop to Paul's writings had accomplished much and yet was in a moral free fall. Sexual immorality was rampant, including homosexuality; graft in political offices was the norm; violence and cruelty were commonplace; the arts featured lewdness and suggested sexual excess. And into the face of this howling moral wasteland, Paul wrote,
Darkened minds + darkened hearts = darkened behavior
Sin has a narcotic effect on persons and cultures. It feels good and is fun for a while, but then it begins to break us down and deaden us to what is good, right, and true. As you deal with moral and ethical darkness, remember that that kind of behavior is merely consistent with darkened, deadened hearts and minds. Lovingly shine the light of God's love and truth on those behaviors, and pray for God to bring about change. Start with yourself. Don't let the culture define your moral standards. Help to keep the church a citadel of proper moral conduct. Make your family a place where you teach and uphold high moral standards.

4:20 But that isn't what you were taught when you learned about Christ.^{NLT} In great contrast to the unbelieving Gentiles (referred to as "they" in the previous verses) stands the word "you" in this verse. The Ephesian believers had been *taught* and had *learned* *about Christ* from Paul himself as well as from other teachers. To know Christ is the greatest knowledge that anyone can have. That knowledge is the truth; that knowledge opposes what the evil world teaches and applauds. Therefore, what the Ephesians and the other believ-

> "To know" is not a mere exercise of the head. Nothing is "known" until it has also passed over into obedience.
>
> *J. A. Motyer*

ers were taught should make all the difference in their lifestyles.

NEW AND IMPROVED

In direct contrast to the preceding description of the unregenerate person, Paul next described the new life of the believer. He wrote of:

- our *new minds:* "But that isn't what you were taught when you learned about Christ. Surely you heard of him and were taught in him in accordance with the truth that is in Jesus. You were taught . . . to be renewed in the spirit of your minds."
- our *new hearts:* "[You were taught] to put off your old self, which is being corrupted by its deceitful desires."
- our *new behavior:* "Clothe yourselves with the new self, created according to the likeness of God in true righteousness and holiness."

From darkened minds, hearts, and behavior, to new ones—this is the stark contrast from the old self to the new. Does your life reflect this contrast, the marks of the new life of the believer? Are there evidences of it in your thinking, desires, will, and behavior?

4:21 Surely you heard of him and were taught in him in accordance with the truth that is in Jesus.[NIV] The phrase translated *heard of him* is literally "heard him," referring to the individual's hearing the call to salvation and responding. This only happened because they had been *taught in him* by those who shared the gospel *in accordance with the truth that is in Jesus.* Jesus is the truth (John 14:6). Paul rarely used the name "Jesus" and generally did so when referring to the death and resurrection of the man Jesus. Here it may not indicate any theological distinction but may merely be a stylistic change. This is the truth that the Ephesians heard and believed. This is the truth that brings salvation.

4:22 You were taught, with regard to your former way of life, to put off your old self, which is being corrupted by its deceitful desires.[NIV] While unbelievers live in darkness and sensuality, believers *were taught* in Christ a whole new manner of living, which must leave behind the *former way of life.* Paul explained that believers must decisively *put off* the *old self.* The "old self" (literally, "old man," also translated "old nature") describes each person before he or she comes to know Christ. The person was enslaved to sin, bound to the world, and without hope. Those who have accepted Christ are still susceptible to temptations and the evils of the sinful nature. Paul does not distinguish between two parts or two natures within a person. The old self describes those areas of rebellion against God. We must forsake this former lifestyle. Like old clothes, we must shed our identification with our sinful past and live as new people. To "put off" that old self will take conscious, daily decisions to remove anything that supports or feeds the old self's desires.

The person's old self *is being corrupted by its deceitful desires* (which Paul described in 4:17-19 above). The verb form "is being corrupted" reveals a continuous process that ends in complete degeneration and death. Like a cancer, the evil nature of the old self spreads and destroys. Christ came to offer each person a new self (4:23-24), but he or she must desire Christ's help to "put off" the old self. As a person takes off an old, dirty garment in exchange for something clean and new, so the believer can take off the old, filthy "self" and exchange it for the clean and pure "self" provided by Christ. The verb "put off" is in the aorist tense, so it describes a definite act. This "putting off" is a once-and-for-all decision when we decide to accept Christ's gift of salvation (2:8-10). Although this putting off of the old takes place at conversion, we must drive out the remaining parts of it day by day. See also Romans 6:6; Colossians 3:5-10; and James 1:21.

> Repentance is primarily a change of moral purpose, a sudden and often violent reversal of the soul's direction.
>
> *A. W. Tozer*

4:23-24 And to be renewed in the spirit of your minds, and to clothe yourselves with the new self, created according to the likeness of God in true righteousness and holiness.[NRSV] We cannot "put off" without also "putting on." Believers must "put off the old self" (4:22), but then they should follow with two specific actions: (1) *to be renewed in the spirit of your minds,* and (2) *to clothe yourselves with the new self.*

The verb "to clothe" (like the verb "to put off" in 4:22) refers to a once-and-for-all action. When believers put off the old self and clothe themselves with the new self, they don't keep on changing back into old clothes once in a while. The old clothes have been thrown away. While we are still on this earth, we will struggle with our old way of life. Paul understood this struggle clearly (see Romans 7:14-25). In explaining these concepts, some

people have wrongly given ...
two equal-but-opposite poles ...
against each other. This is no...
words. Christ sees his people ...
renewed," describes a continu...
exchanged, but the process of ...
is a continual daily process. Tr...
and results in renewed behavior.

How are believers "to be rene...
minds"? They must:

- be involved in activities that re...
  4:8-9);
- desire to pattern themselves afte... ...orld (Romans
  12:2);
- study and apply God's Word so that it changes their behavior
  from within (2 Timothy 3:15-16).

As just noted, the tense of the verb indicates a daily act. The
"spirit" refers to the Holy Spirit controlling the believers' minds,
or it may refer to the spiritual side of each person's mind-set,
which is where renewal must begin (Romans 12:2; Colossians
3:10). Most likely, the meaning may be a combination of both,
for the human spirit can only be renewed by the divine Spirit.
(See also 2 Corinthians 5:17; Galatians 6:15; Colossians 3:10;
Titus 3:5.)

This *new self* with which believers are *to clothe* themselves is
a new creation, *created according to the likeness of God in true
righteousness and holiness.* This new self (literally, "new man")
is the new relationship we have with Christ that gives us a new
orientation to life. The new self is *according to the likeness of
God* with the characteristics of *true righteousness and holiness.*
We have a right relationship with God
that results in right behavior, creates an
aversion to sin, and prompts us to
devote ourselves to his service. These
qualities are "true," meaning they cannot be faked. This is totally opposite of
the old way of living characterized by
sin and corruption. Finally, the new self

> However holy or
> Christlike a Christian may
> become, he is still in the
> condition of "being
> changed."
> *John R. W. Stott*

refers not to a split in one's personality; instead, it pictures the
new direction, attitude, and mind-set away from self and toward
God and his will.

**4:25 So then, putting away falsehood, let all of us speak the truth
to our neighbors, for we are members of one another.**NRSV

ter of the new self will lead to specific ways
se believers in the church exhibit "true righ-
d holiness" (4:24), they must put away *falsehood.*
refer to various forms of falsehood—anything that
ns to the old lifestyle and is not part of Christ's truth.
ke putting off the old self and replacing it with the new self,
so believers put off falsehood and put on the willingness to
speak the truth. This is a quote from Zechariah 8:16. This reference in the Septuagint (Greek version of the Old Testament)
says speak the truth "to" *(pros)*, while Paul said speak the truth
"with" *(meta).* The change in focus lies in the following clause:
for we are members of one another. Paul stressed our mutual
responsibility. Because we are members of one another in
Christ's body, our words and actions must not be destructive
to the body. Lying to each other disrupts unity by creating
conflicts and destroying trust. It tears down relationships and
leads to open warfare in a church. Truthfulness, however,
opens the door to understanding. To maintain unity, the believers
must be completely truthful with one another.

4:26-27 **"In your anger do not sin": Do not let the sun go down
while you are still angry, and do not give the devil a foothold.**[NIV] Another characteristic of the old self that has to be put
off is bad temper, or a lifestyle characterized by anger. The
words "in your anger do not sin" are quoted from Psalm 4:4.
The Bible doesn't tell us that we shouldn't feel angry, but it
points out that it is important to handle our anger properly. We
must not indulge our angry feelings or let them lead to pride,
hatred, or self-righteousness. Jesus Christ became angry at the
merchants in the temple, but this was righteous anger and did
not lead him to sin. Believers must follow Jesus' example. We
ought to reserve our anger for when we see God dishonored
or people wronged. If we get angry, we must do so without
sinning. To do this, we should deal with our anger before the
sun goes down. According to Deuteronomy, sunset was the
time by which wrongs against God and against others should
be made right (Deuteronomy 24:13, 15). Anger that is allowed
to smolder and burn over time can eventually burst into flame
and *give the devil a foothold,* causing people to sin as they
become bitter and resentful. We should resist the devil (James
4:7). Satan can use our anger against one another to destroy
our unity and our love. It is so much better to deal with the situation immediately; perhaps the previous admonition to lovingly
speak the truth can solve the problem.

DON'T GET BURNED!
If vented thoughtlessly, anger can hurt others and destroy relationships. If kept inside, it can cause us to become bitter and destroy us from within. Paul tells us to deal with our anger immediately in a way that builds relationships rather than destroys them. If we nurse our anger, we will give Satan an opportunity to divide us. Anger must be dealt with as quickly as possible. Used correctly, anger can motivate us to right a wrong, redress a grievance, correct an injustice. Used improperly, it can burn us and everyone else around us. Are you angry with someone right now? What can you do to resolve your differences? Don't let the day end before you begin working on mending your relationship.

4:28 If you are a thief, stop stealing. Begin using your hands for honest work, and then give generously to others in need.NLT In most cases, a reference to stealing or to *a thief* in the New Testament concerns a bandit or a person who engages in stealing as a livelihood. Paul explained that such a person who became a believer had to "put off" that old lifestyle and make a change, turning to *honest work* in order to make a living. Stealing and idleness go together; thus, Paul's charge was not only to stop stealing but also to begin honest work. In addition, slaves were often prone to stealing from the households they served; many slaves became Christians, and Paul may have been speaking to them. All believers should work hard, do their part in the community, hold their own, and not expect anyone else to support them.

Even then, the Christian's goal for his or her labor differs from the world's. We work not to enrich ourselves, but so that we can *give generously to others in need.* Giving is at the heart of Christianity. We hold lightly to our possessions because we have our treasure in heaven (Matthew 6:19-21; Romans 12:13; 2 Corinthians 8–9).

4:29 Do not let any unwholesome talk come out of your mouths, but only what is helpful for building others up according to their needs, that it may benefit those who listen.NIV Believers must also be careful about what they say. As part of Christ's body, filled with his righteousness and holiness, they must *not let any unwholesome talk come out* of their mouths. "Unwholesome" means corrupt, insipid, worthless (such as gossip and slander), and it includes foul talk (such as coarse language). Such speech is worthless, spreads worthlessness, and leads hearers to think about worthless matters. Not only should our speech be kept clean and truthful, but we should also speak *only what is helpful for building others up* *according to their needs.* We must be sensitive to the situation and the needs of anyone with whom we converse, and we must be wise in choosing our words, for even good words, unless used appropriately, can be destructive instead of useful. We should not speak vaguely in words that could fit a thousand different occasions. Rather, our words should be genuine and specifically suited to the present person, time, and place. Our speech should edify, not tear down. Unless we help the other person, our words will be meaningless. What we say can *benefit those who listen.* God can work through our words to help others and bring his grace to them.

CROSS WORDS

Words count. The words we say to one another can be a powerful force for good, for building each other up. Conversely, they can be just as powerfully destructive, tearing us down. Think back to when you were young: What kinds of words do you remember the significant adults in your life using toward you? Were they positive, encouraging words that built you up and made you feel valuable and worthwhile? Or did you hear more terms like "loser," "worthless," "stupid"? The memories either bring smiles or cause pain. Your words have the same effect on those around you, especially on children and young people. Take a mental inventory of your speech. Do your words build up or tear down? With God's help, commit to being the kind of person whose words encourage and edify others.

4:30 And do not grieve the Holy Spirit of God, by whom you were sealed for the day of redemption.NKJV That the Spirit can be saddened or grieved points to the personality of the Spirit. The Holy Spirit is a person who can be saddened by the way we live. Paul has already explained that the Holy Spirit's power within gives new life to believers. While we continue to battle with our sinful nature, we should be living for Christ each day. To refuse to do so, to constantly give in to lying, anger, stealing, and foul talk is to *grieve the Holy Spirit of God.* "Grieving" is different from "stifling" the Holy Spirit (1 Thessalonians 5:19), which has to do with stifling prophecy. Paul's reference to the Holy Spirit brings to mind Isaiah 63:10 and reminds believers that the Holy Spirit binds them together in the body. When believers quarrel and hurt one another, they distress the Spirit. Because the Holy Spirit controls and guides speech, praise, prophecy, and tongues, we offend him when we use them improperly. (See also Acts 7:51; 1 Thessalonians 4:8.)

Paul reminded the readers that the Holy Spirit within them gives both a privilege and a responsibility. Their responsibility is to not disappoint him by the way they live; their privilege is their promised future, for through the presence of the Spirit, they *were sealed for the day of redemption.* The seal of the Holy Spirit upon a believer marks that believer as God's property until the day he or she is completely redeemed. It connotes the protected status of the believer. (For more on this sealing, see commentary on 1:13-14.)

> How would you like to live with somebody who was everlastingly grieving your heart by his conduct?
>
> *G. Campbell Morgan*

THE HURT

Paul gives us a surprising reason for choosing the right over the wrong: so that we don't grieve the Holy Spirit—not just so that we don't hurt one another, but also so that we do not sadden God the Spirit. What a powerful incentive to do what is right and avoid what is evil! What a privilege and responsibility to know that our actions have that kind of effect on God. How do your words, thoughts, and behavior impact him?

4:31 Get rid of all bitterness, rage and anger, brawling and slander, along with every form of malice.NIV The sins listed in this verse picture the former way of life, the old self (4:22). None of these attitudes and activities have any place in the believers' Holy Spirit-filled life; indeed, they foster dissension today and are the opposite of how believers should be characterized (see 4:32). In their lives and in their churches, the believers must *get rid of:*

- *Bitterness*—a spirit that refuses reconciliation.
- *Rage*—outbursts of anger or quick temper for selfish reasons. This could mean continual and uncontrolled behavior.
- *Anger*—a continuous attitude of hatred that remains bottled up within. This could refer to what is under the surface, while "rage" refers to what bursts out. Anger would destroy harmony and unity among believers.
- *Brawling*—loud self-assertions of angry people determined to make their grievances known.
- *Slander*—destroying another person's good reputation by lying, gossiping, spreading rumors, etc. Malice often manifests itself through slander. This defamation of character destroys human relationships.
- *Malice*—doing evil despite the good that has been received. This word is a general term referring to an evil force that destroys relationships, and it can mean anything from trouble to wickedness. It is a deliberate attempt to harm another person. Thus, *every form of* malice must be destroyed.

4:32 And be kind to one another, tenderhearted, forgiving one another, even as God in Christ forgave you.^{NKJV} The previous way of life must be put off (4:31) and the new life put on. Believers ought to *be kind to one another.* Kindness means acting charitably and benevolently toward others, as God has done toward us. Kindness takes the initiative in responding generously to others' needs. The Psalms and writings of the prophets say much about God's kindness. Because believers have received kindness, we ought to act with kindness toward others.

The word for *tenderhearted* is also translated "compassionate." Compassion is genuine sensitivity and heartfelt sympathy for the needs of others. Compassion characterizes God.

Believers must also be constantly *forgiving one another.* In what way? *Even as God in Christ forgave you.* Though Christ has bridged the gap between us and God so that we are forgiven once and for all, we only experience God's forgiveness in personal, practical ways as we learn to forgive others from day to day. None of us has experienced as great a wrong against ourselves as that which we have all done to God (Matthew 18:33). God had to give up his only Son to forgive us; we have nothing to give up but our selfish natures and our unwillingness to forgive those who have wronged us. Christ taught this law of forgiveness (Matthew 6:14-15; 18:35; Mark 11:25). We also see it in the Lord's Prayer—"Forgive us our debts, as we forgive our debtors" (Matthew 6:12 NKJV). God does not forgive us *because* we forgive others, but solely because of his great mercy. As we come to understand his mercy, however, we will want to be like him. Having received forgiveness, we will pass it on to others. Those who are unwilling to forgive have not patterned their lives after Christ, who was willing to forgive even those who crucified him (Luke 23:34).

5:1 Therefore be imitators of God as dear children.^{NKJV} Just as children imitate their parents, we should *be imitators of God.* His great love for us led him to sacrifice his Son so that we might live. We imitate God by following his example in Christ, emulating his attributes in our lives (see 1 Peter 2:21). The following verse (5:2) shows that Christ's example of forgiveness should be the pattern we follow. The word "be" means "become." Paul understood that this is a process. Because of our relationship with God through Christ and the power given us through the Spirit, we are to become Godlike in our characteristics and obedient disciples in our lifestyles.

IMPRINTED
Behavioral scientists have discovered an interesting phenomenon
called "imprinting" in the early development of some animals. At
certain critical stages, whatever other animal, object, or person
the young animal is exposed to is taken to be its "parent." If a
young goose is "imprinted" with a dog, the gosling will see the
dog as its mother. Paul says that such imprinting should happen
in Christian growth. We should walk so closely with Jesus that
he imprints on us his nature: loving, serving, sacrificing, pleasing
to God the Father. Stay close to him through Bible study, prayer,
fellowship, and evangelism so that you are always in a position
to be transformed into his image.

**5:2 And walk in love, as Christ also has loved us and given Himself
for us, an offering and a sacrifice to God for a sweet-smelling
aroma.**^{NKJV} The verb "walk" continues the thought from 5:1, that
we must imitate God. How we "walk" should be characterized by
our oneness with him. Paul explained that we are to walk *in love*.
Our love for others should be of the same kind that Christ showed
to us—a love that goes beyond affection to self-sacrificing service.
Christ loved us so much that he gave *Himself for us* as *an offering
and a sacrifice to God.* Christ gave himself in death as a sacrifice
on our behalf. The words "offering" and "sacrifice" are really
synonymous, although the first word generally indicates a gift and
the second always designates a slain animal (as in the sacrifices of
the Old Testament). The *sweet-smelling aroma* relates to the accept-
ability of the sacrifice. God was not bound to accept any offering
(Genesis 4:5); he did so only on the basis of the attitude of the giver.
This focuses on God's pleasure with Christ's sacrifice. Because
God accepted Christ's sacrifice, we who believe are acceptable
to God. Because of this, our love ought to also be self-sacrificial.
Jesus had told his disciples, "Love one another as I have loved
you" (John 15:12 NKJV).

**5:3 But among you there must not be even a hint of sexual immo-
rality, or of any kind of impurity, or of greed, because these
are improper for God's holy people.**^{NIV} In 4:17-24 Paul
described, in general terms, the putting off of the old self and the
putting on of the new; in 4:25-31, he described particular sins
of speech and personal animosities. He continued here in 5:3-4,
further describing actions that are unsuitable among the Christian
community. *Sexual immorality* includes any kind of sexual per-
version. That *there must not be even a hint* of these sins includes
what Jesus said in Matthew 5—that even thinking immoral
thoughts is as bad as committing them. Sexual immorality was

tolerated in the pagan Roman society (see Romans 1:24-32), but it should not exist in the Christian community.

Neither should there be *any kind of impurity.* As in 4:19, "impurity" is aligned with a lifestyle bent on fulfilling every indulgence, so the focus in this verse is probably on sexual indulgence.

"Greed" refers to an inordinate desire for anything—wanting something so much that one sacrifices everything to get it. Again, this verse may focus on sexual immorality and indulgence—the greed to have what one should not have. Such desires are idolatrous.

"No hint" of these sins should be found in the church *because these are improper for God's holy people.* God's people should exhibit his attributes. These activities are the opposite of what God desires from his people.

NOT EVEN A HINT!
If you have ever owned a big dog like a German shepherd, a Doberman pinscher, or a Rottweiler (or know someone who has), you know how important it is to make sure the dog knows who is the master. Kept under control, a dog like that can be a tremendous source of joy and a benefit to its family's welfare and security. Out of control, the dog can be a dangerous beast. That's why its owner must be very strict with it. On the other hand, an out-of-control Chihuahua doesn't present a serious danger. The sins mentioned in these verses are powerful and hard to control once they get a foothold in our lives. That's why the language is so harsh: "Among you there must not be even a hint of sexual immorality . . . impurity . . . greed," etc. Paul knew how hard it is to control lust, greed, vulgar language, and idolatry. Like a good trainer, he wanted the believers to get control of these beasts and keep them under control. How do you deal with these and other temptations? Be relentless in your obedience training.

5:4 Entirely out of place is obscene, silly, and vulgar talk; but instead, let there be thanksgiving.^{NRSV} Obscenity and coarse joking are so common that we begin to take them for granted. Paul cautioned, however, that improper language should have no place in a Christian's conversation because it does not reflect God's gracious presence in us. This use of language by believers sometimes stems from their desire to remain inconspicuous by sounding like the people who surround them. Principle is sacrificed to the convenience of the particular occasion.

Throughout this section, Paul told the believers not to just get rid of some types of attitudes and activities but to replace them with others. So here, the *obscene, silly, and vulgar talk* is to be

replaced by *thanksgiving.* In this way, our words will build up
and benefit others (4:29). Giving thanks brings about the real joy
of the spirit that the worldly people try to achieve with their style
of humor and communication. Paul did not mean that all other
talk is vulgar; rather, he commanded against the foolish and
vulgar talk that harms the spiritual life.

**5:5 For of this you can be sure: No immoral, impure or greedy
person—such a man is an idolater—has any inheritance in
the kingdom of Christ and of God.**[NIV] Immorality, impurity, and
greed (described in 5:3) are compared to idolatry because those
who consistently engage in these types of activities are idolaters.
Because they have allowed their desires to run their lives, those
desires are their gods. Anyone who has made anything more
important than God has no *inheritance in the kingdom of Christ
and of God.* In the Greek, the words "of Christ and of God"
emphasize the complete unity of the Father and the Son, consistent with the doctrine that Christ is completely God (John 10:30).
Sin, no matter what its form or category, separates people from
God. Unrepentance leaves people without hope and without
inheritance. Only by forsaking sin, accepting Christ's sacrifice,
and allowing him to be Lord of our lives can we believers obtain
our inheritance in God's glorious kingdom (1:14, 18).

BE WARY
Paul does not forbid all contact with unbelievers. Jesus taught
his followers to befriend sinners and lead them to him (Luke
5:30-32). Instead, Paul wrote against the lifestyle of people
who make excuses for bad behavior and recommend its
practice to others—whether they are in the church or outside
of it. Such people quickly pollute the church and endanger its
unity and purpose. We must befriend unbelievers if we are to
lead them to Christ, but we must be wary of those who are
viciously evil, immoral, or opposed to all that Christianity stands
for. Such people are more likely to influence us for evil than we
are to influence them for good.

Ephesians 5:6-33

5:6-7 Let no one deceive you with empty words, for because of these things the wrath of God comes on those who are disobedient. Therefore do not be associated with them.^{NRSV} This verse builds on 4:14. False teachers had begun infiltrating the early church, teaching that "freedom in Christ" meant freedom "from" laws and rules, freedom to live as one pleased. In 5:3-5, Paul mentioned various activities and attitudes that are "entirely out of place" (5:4 NRSV) among believers. The false teachers taught their false doctrines, probably even trying to make evil seem less serious by saying that it was natural to indulge in impurity and might even be good for us at times (5:3), that it was useful to society to go after money and possessions ("greed," 5:3), and that God would not punish clever wit, even if it was in the form of obscenity and vulgarity (5:4). The false teachers made up a doctrine that allowed for sinful lifestyles. Paul did not want the believers to be deceived by their *empty words.* Such words have no weight and no depth—they are "empty" because they are lies.

Paul gave similar warnings in many of his letters because false teachers were a constant threat to the new believers. In fact, Paul had told the Ephesian elders:

- *And now beware! Be sure that you feed and shepherd God's flock—his church, purchased with his blood—over whom the Holy Spirit has appointed you as elders. I know full well that false teachers, like vicious wolves, will come in among you after I leave, not sparing the flock. Even some of you will distort the truth in order to draw a following. Watch out! Remember the three years I was with you—my constant watch and care over you night and day, and my many tears for you.* (Acts 20:28-31 NLT)

The "vicious wolves" in the Acts passage quoted above refer to the false teachers that would come and distort the truth. Paul continued to warn the believers in Ephesus against the deceptions that would be placed before them—the tiny distortions, the half-truths, the plausible arguments that were, in reality, lies. The believers should be on guard and not be deceived *for because of these things the wrath of God comes on those who are disobedient.* Empty words had already aroused God's anger (the word "comes" is in the present tense, indicating a present reality). The permissive activities described in 5:3-5 (and those who espouse such license) arouse God's anger because they come from the enemy, "the ruler of the kingdom of the air, the spirit who is now at work in those who are disobedient" (2:2 NIV). Those who thought they could continue in sin as a part of their "freedom" would discover that they were never free but were all the time enslaved to their sin. And they would face God's wrath both in the present and in the future.

Therefore, because of God's wrath on sin and because sinful activities are incompatible with life in Christ's kingdom, Paul told the believers to *not be associated with* people who pretend Christianity and practice permissiveness. This "association" refers to joining them in their sinful activities or in justifying sin. To do so would be to mock the sacrifice Christ made in order to take away sin. True believers have been saved "from" that old self in order to "put on the new self, created to be like God in true righteousness and holiness" (4:24 NIV).

LOVE AND FEAR
Most would agree that love is a better motivator than fear. It is better to do something for someone out of love than out of fear of the consequences for not doing it. Obviously, this applies to our Christian conduct as well, but Paul felt the need to address the negative side of obedience: what happens to those who disobey. He wrote that the wrath of God "comes on those who are disobedient." The message could be paraphrased this way: Obey God and serve one another out of love. But when for whatever reason love doesn't motivate you, let fear do it—the fear of standing exposed to God's wrath. In a perfect world, we need only love. In this world, sometimes godly fear is called for. Examine your motives and learn to listen to the love of God so you need not fear His wrath.

5:8-10 For you were once darkness, but now you are light in the Lord.NIV There can be no clearer distinction between the new life and the old life than to compare them to light and darkness. Light and darkness cannot coexist, so a life redeemed by the blood of Christ and brought into the light of his truth must not continue in the darkness of a sinful lifestyle. Paul had already described unbelievers as "darkened in their understanding" due to ignorance, hard-heartedness, and lack of sensitivity (4:18-19). This darkness is part

of every believer's past; all Christians *were once darkness.* But when
they heard the gospel message and received salvation through Jesus
Christ, they became *light in the Lord.* Christians are not merely
"enlightened" to God's truth; they are also filled with light.

**Live as children of light (for the fruit of the light consists in
all goodness, righteousness and truth).**^{NIV} "Children of" is a
Hebrew idiom for "those who are characterized by a quality."
Christians, as God's children, are "children of light" because they
characterize God, who is light (1 John 1:5). As such, believers
should *live* as God's children ought to live, reflecting the light of
his holiness and truth. The *fruit of the light*—that is, the natural
outcome of such a lifestyle—is *goodness, righteousness, and
truth* (the opposites of the characteristics described in 4:25-29
and 5:3-5; see also Galatians 5:22-23). In other words, believers
who live in God's light are above reproach morally, spiritually,
and ethically. Then they reflect God's goodness to others. Jesus
stressed this truth in the Sermon on the Mount (Matthew 5:15-16).

LIGHT AND DARK
Paul contrasts light (the Christian life) with darkness (life
outside of Christ). Think for a moment about the properties of
light: Light illuminates; light separates (from darkness); light
causes growth; light exposes. If your life were exposed to the
light of God's truth and holiness, what would it reveal? That
would be a rather unpleasant prospect for the saintliest person.
All of us have dark corners—attitudes, thoughts, desires—that
we would not want illuminated before God or anyone else.
Thankfully, the light of God's holiness shines through the filter
of his grace. Reflect for a moment on those thoughts and
deeds you would not want that light to reveal . . . and thank
God that he has mercifully covered those sins with the cross.
Take steps to remove any immoral behavior from your life.

And find out what pleases the Lord.^{NIV} Every believer is
responsible to *find out what pleases the Lord*—how he or she
ought to "live in the light." Thus, each person must study God's
Word, pray, and seek counsel in order to *find out* how God
would have him or her act in every situation. This "finding out"
naturally goes with "living out" because the knowledge must
be put into practical use—doing what God calls us to do in
every situation every day. Paul had written to the Romans, "Do
not conform any longer to the pattern of this world, but be transformed by the renewing of your mind. Then you will be able to
test and approve what God's will is—his good, pleasing and
perfect will" (Romans 12:2 NIV). Clearly, the Christian life is

meant to be both an inner renewal and an outward change of habit and lifestyle.

5:11 Take no part in the unfruitful works of darkness, but instead expose them.^{NRSV} Light and darkness cannot coexist, so children of the light (5:8) must *take no part in the unfruitful works of darkness.* Believers' lives are characterized by the "fruit" of "goodness, righteousness and truth" (5:9), but the *works of darkness* (sin and evil) are *unfruitful* because they end in death and decay (see Romans 6:21). Thus, believers must separate themselves from sin, having no part of it. This does not mean that believers must be separate from unbelievers, but they must "take no part" in their sinful actions. It is important to avoid activities that result in sin, but we must go even further. Paul instructed believers to *expose* these deeds because our silence may be interpreted as approval. Just as the light shines into darkness and exposes what is hidden, so the light of Christ, through a believer, should shine into the darkness of sin and expose it for what it is. God needs people who will take an active and vocal stand against sin and permissiveness in all its forms (see Leviticus 19:17). Christians must lovingly speak out for what is true and right.

EXPOSED
Some things love the dark. Have you ever walked into a room in the middle of the night and turned on the light, only to catch a glimpse of a cockroach or other pest scurrying for cover? Roaches, rats, and other unwelcome intruders hate the light. They run from it as fast as possible. That's not a very flattering image, but it is the way Paul describes people who don't follow Christ. Their deeds, he says, are shameful even to talk about. They need to have the light of the gospel shined on them, exposing them for what they really are. Are you willing to take a stand, calling darkness and evil what they really are, and walk in the light? Don't do anything in secret that you would be ashamed of in broad daylight.

5:12-14 For it is shameful even to mention what such people do secretly.^{NRSV} While believers should stand for the truth, they ought not get caught up in empty talk and gossip about the *shameful* actions of sinful people. We should not promote or dignify sin by even so much as discussing it.

But everything exposed by the light becomes visible, for it is light that makes everything visible.^{NIV} When we bring a light into the darkness, it exposes everything for what it is. Nothing can hide from the light. Paul described the revealing power of light as he

explained that *everything exposed by the light becomes visible.*
Light is seen as piercing through darkness. Believers are the "rays"
of that light. By our actions (5:8-12), we become instruments of
light, exposing the dark acts of sin. *It is light that makes everything
visible* refers to believers' mission. Believers who shine out in a
dark world will expose evil. Their mission is to invite unbelievers
to renounce their life of sin and come into Christ's light so that
they, too, can become "light in the Lord" (5:8).

**Therefore it says, "Sleeper, awake! Rise from the dead, and
Christ will shine on you."**NRSV This is not a direct quote from
Scripture but may have been taken from a hymn well known to the
Ephesians. The hymn could have been part of a baptismal hymn
that was sung by the congregation for a new convert when he or
she emerged from the baptismal waters. For the new believer, coming out of spiritual death is like awaking from sleep, and coming
into spiritual life is like greeting the sunshine—who is Christ. The
hymn seems to have been based on Isaiah 26:19; 51:17; 52:1; and
60:1. As the prophets appealed to Israel to awaken from its state of
darkness and death, so Paul was appealing to the Ephesians to
wake up, stay alert, and realize the dangerous condition into which
some of them had been slipping by listening to false teachings.

**5:15-16 Be very careful, then, how you live—not as unwise but as wise,
making the most of every opportunity, because the days are
evil.**NIV Because of believers' responsibility to live as children of
light (5:8) and to expose evil, they must *be very careful* how they
live. Their lives must please God (5:10), and they must conduct
themselves before unbelievers so as to shine with Christ and draw
others to him. Paul encouraged the believers to live *not as unwise
but as wise.* In other words, they must take their knowledge of
Christ and apply it to their everyday lives and be especially aware
of their conduct with unbelievers. Paul wrote to the Colossians,
"Be wise in the way you act toward outsiders" (Colossians 4:5
NIV). Wisdom has been made available to them; they need only
ask for it (1:17; James 1:5; 3:17).

The Greek phrase for *making the most of every opportunity*
conveys the idea of "buying from time" or "redeeming time." The
believers should carefully use their time, making use of opportunities for doing good (see Galatians 6:10). This implies that we
should not allow ourselves to be controlled by our circumstances;
rather, we should make use of time as a valuable commodity or
resource, as a master does with his servant. We should not read
into this verse that God expects or condones workaholics. God
has given us periods of both work and rest. We must never find in

Scripture an excuse to neglect our physical needs or the needs of our families. Why be so concerned about using every opportunity to help draw people from darkness to light? *Because the days are evil,* wrote Paul. He was communicating his sense of urgency because of evil's pervasiveness.

IT'S TIME
Make a quick mental list of the things you really value. Undoubtedly your list would include your loved ones, your home, your church, and perhaps a few other possessions. Would it also include your *time?* Paul's admonition to live carefully, "making the most of every opportunity," is a reminder of the preciousness of time. Think about it. If someone takes away your money, you may not like it, but you can earn more money. If someone or something takes away your job or even your house, it might be very difficult, but you can get another job or house. But if something takes your time and wastes it, you can never get it back. Those hours or days are gone, never to be retrieved. That makes time a very valuable thing indeed. What are you doing with the time God has given you? Are you "making the most of every opportunity," allowing him to use you and your time as he sees fit?

5:17 So do not be foolish, but understand what the will of the Lord is.NRSV Believers must not waste their time being *foolish.* We have a job to do, and our lives must reflect our motivation and our goal—to serve our Lord, to share his gospel message, and to be ready for his kingdom. We should not be foolish and silly but instead show that we *understand what the will of the Lord is.* We have not only intellectually comprehended God's will, as taught in his Word, but we are also continually learning and growing in our understanding as we walk with him. What is the will of the Lord? Ultimately, it is our sanctification (1 Thessalonians 4:3). As his servants, we ought to do everything we can to work toward his will for us. In one of his parables, Jesus said, "That servant who knows his master's will and does not get ready or does not do what his master wants will be beaten with many blows" (Luke 12:47 NIV). How do we live this out? We have been given an example in the life of our Savior, Jesus Christ.

5:18 Do not get drunk on wine, which leads to debauchery. Instead, be filled with the Spirit.NIV These words should be considered in light of the whole section (4:17–5:20) in which Paul has contrasted the "before and after" of the believers' lives. Getting drunk with wine was associated with the old way of life and its selfish desires, which Paul has already condemned as corrupt (4:22). Some have

suggested that there had been misconduct in the church or during
the celebration of the Lord's Table, a problem Paul addressed in
Corinth (see 1 Corinthians 11:21). Yet there is little evidence that
the problems in Corinth were widespread. Another view is that
drunkenness was a problem in this culture, as well as being part of
some pagan worship celebrations. Most likely, the believers already
knew that drunkenness should not be a part of their Christian lives.
Paul wrote these words in order to deliberately contrast drunkenness
with the infilling of the Spirit in the same way that he contrasted
those in darkness and those living in the light (5:8). In Romans
13:12-13 and 1 Thessalonians 5:6-8, Paul also associated drunkenness with darkness, and sobriety with light.

Getting drunk *leads to debauchery*—the word refers to a drunk
person's being out of control, as well as to the person's wasteful-
ness (of resources and of life itself). These have no place in the
lives of believers. Besides, we don't need alcohol, according to
Paul, for we are *filled with the Spirit.* Paul contrasted getting drunk
with wine, which produces a temporary "high," to being filled with
the Spirit, which produces lasting joy. "We were all given the one
Spirit to drink" (1 Corinthians 12:13 NIV). The focus of Paul's
words here is not so much the prohibition against drunkenness, for
the believers probably already understood that, but his urging that
they continually be filled by and live in the Spirit. When a person is
drunk, everyone can tell. His or her actions make it obvious. In like
manner, our lives should be so completely under the Spirit's control
that our actions and words show beyond a doubt that we are filled
with the presence of God's Holy Spirit.

WHO'S IN CHARGE?
Although Ephesians 5:18 is often quoted in support of
antidrinking efforts, the underlying issue goes deeper than
whether or not to drink alcohol. The more important concern is,
what—or who—is going to be in control of your life? Either the
Holy Spirit is, or something else is. And whatever else it may
be, it's a poor substitute. Being filled with alcohol can make you
lose control and do stupid things. Being filled with the Holy
Spirit *gives* you self-control (Galatians 5:23) and helps you
worship God and serve others.

The words "be filled" are a command for all believers, yet believers
do not manufacture it—God fills believers with his Spirit when
they profess faith in Jesus Christ as Savior. Paul was not suggesting
that the believers in Ephesus needed to "get filled"; rather, he was
saying, "Since you are already filled with the Spirit, keep on like

that." The words are also in the present tense, indicating constant replenishment with the Spirit—believers are not "once-and-for-all" filled but rather are continually being filled with the Spirit as they continue to walk with God.

5:19-20 Speak to one another with psalms, hymns and spiritual songs. Sing and make music in your heart to the Lord, always giving thanks to God the Father for everything, in the name of our Lord Jesus Christ.[NIV] Just as drunkenness is evidence of too much wine, so Spirit-filled worship should be evidence of the Holy Spirit's presence. From this exhortation came much of the style of historic corporate Christian worship that is still a part of our worship today. Believers can encourage one another and give praise to God through music. Paul mentioned *psalms,* such as the psalms of the Old Testament, as well as new ones written in the old style. The psalms were usually accompanied by a harp. *Hymns and spiritual songs* were written by the believers and could be used in praise to God. Some fragments of these hymns may exist in some of Paul's letters (see Philippians 2:5-11; Colossians 1:15-18; 1 Timothy 3:16). Although the early Christians had access to the Old Testament and freely used it, they did not yet have the New Testament or any other Christian books to study. Their stories and teachings about Christ were sometimes set to music to make them easier to memorize and pass on from person to person. *Spiritual songs* may refer to either charismatic singing in the Spirit or to songs previously composed and sung spontaneously. Believers are to be full of the Holy Spirit when they sing. Grounded in God's Word and correct doctrine, music can be an important part of Christian worship and education.

UNDER THE INFLUENCE
The effects of alcohol are obvious. What happens when we are under the influence of the Holy Spirit? In these verses, Paul lists three by-products of the Spirit's influence in our lives: speaking, singing, and giving thanks. When the Holy Spirit controls us, we "speak to one another with psalms, hymns and spiritual songs." We "sing and make music in our hearts to the Lord." And we "[give] thanks to God the Father for everything, in the name of our Lord Jesus Christ." Paul did not intend to suggest that we only discuss religious matters, but that whatever we do or say should be permeated with an attitude of thankfulness to God and encouragement toward each other. Instead of whining and complaining—which our culture has raised to an art form—we are to focus on the goodness of God and his mercies toward us. Which is more characteristic of your words and attitudes?

Paul encouraged the believers to *sing and make music* that comes from the *heart* and offer it *to the Lord.* The singing should be a genuine representation of one's beliefs and feelings—the "heart" referring to the whole being. This makes a contrast between the music of Christians, sung together in praise to God, and the music of unbelievers, done purely for entertainment or self-praise. The primary focus of our singing is to give thanks to God the Father in the name of our Lord Jesus Christ.

WIVES AND HUSBANDS / 5:21-33

Paul presented concepts governing household behavior. Household codes were common among Jewish and Greek communities. As Christianity spread, it aroused suspicion. Tensions grew between Christians and the rest of society. This required Christians to have high standards for their behavior. Paul outlined God's plan for Christian behavior in the home.

5:21 Submit to one another out of reverence for Christ.[NIV] This is the last participial phrase flowing out of being filled with the Spirit and functions to introduce verses 22-33. People often misunderstand the concept of submitting to another person. It does not mean becoming totally passive. Christ—at whose name "every knee should bow, in heaven and on earth and under the earth" (Philippians 2:10 NIV)—submitted his will to the Father, and we honor Christ by following his example. When we submit to God, we become more willing to obey his command to submit to others, that is, to subordinate our rights to theirs. In Paul's day, women, children, and slaves were to submit to the head of the family—slaves would submit until they were freed, male children until they grew up, and women and girls their whole lives. Paul emphasized the equality of all believers in Christ (Galatians 3:28), but he counseled all believers to submit to one another by choice. This kind of mutual submission preserves order and harmony.

Submission provides evidence that we have Spirit-controlled relationships, and it requires the Holy Spirit's guidance and restraint (4:2-3). In the church, the believers should be willing to learn from, serve, give to, or be corrected by others in the fellowship. Such submission can allow growth both individually and corporately as the believers seek to follow Christ. Our motives should be "reverence" (literally, "fear") for Christ. We should not treat one another rightly just because it is expected or because we will be well regarded but because one day we must give account to Christ of how we have lived.

SUBMISSION
This verse acts as a hinge between the preceding verses that deal with wisdom and living under the influence of the Holy Spirit, and the following verses, which consider the relationships between husbands and wives and Christ and the church. In 5:21, Paul says that the one who is filled with the Spirit not only reflects God's goodness in speech and attitudes but also manifests it in willingness to submit to others out of reverence for Christ.

Submission often has unpleasant implications for modern Christians, perhaps because this principle has been abused in the past and has been used to justify overbearing and self-serving behavior. But Jesus was willing to submit to the will of his Father and to the agonies of the cross. "Submission" is not a bad word. How do you respond to the idea of submitting to others? Are you willing to place the interests and desires of others ahead of your own in Jesus' name?

5:22-24 **Wives, submit to your husbands as to the Lord. For the husband is the head of the wife as Christ is the head of the church, his body, of which he is the Savior. Now as the church submits to Christ, so also wives should submit to their husbands in everything.**[NIV] Submission in the church should follow from submission in the home. The home, the foundation for relationships and personal growth, must be an example of peaceful submission. In a marriage relationship, both husband and wife are called to submit. The relationships between husbands and wives are a microcosm of the larger picture of church relationships.

> The best thing a woman can do for her husband is to make it easy for him to do the will of God.
> *Elisabeth Elliot Gren*

Paul spoke first to the *wives,* explaining that they were to *submit* voluntarily to their husbands *as to the Lord.* The words "as to the Lord" mean "as is fitting to the Lord." This does not mean that the husband is "lord" over the wife. Our concept of submission must come from that which exists between Christ and the church: Christ loves the church, and she submits to him. We must not base it on either a feminist or chauvinist view. Christian marriage involves mutual submission, subordinating our personal desires for the good of the loved one and submitting ourselves to Christ as Lord. The wife's submission to her husband is one way that she can demonstrate her submission to Christ. She does this voluntarily out of love for her husband and for Christ.

Paul explained that *the husband is the head of the wife as*

Christ is the head of the church. In other words, the husband is
the spiritual head of the family, and his wife should acknowledge
his leadership. "Head" normally means leader, ruler, or authority
as in 1 Corinthians 11:3, where God is described as the head of
Christ, Christ is the head of man, and
man is the head of woman. Some scholars have debated that "head" should be
taken as the source rather than the
authority, but such an interpretation

> A man of quality is never
> threatened by a woman
> of equality.   *Jill Briscoe*

seems to be out of line with other Greek and Roman household
codes. Real spiritual leadership involves service and sacrifice.
Christ as *head of the church* is also its *Savior.* Christ gave his life
for the church. So, *as the church submits to Christ, so also wives
should submit to their husbands in everything.* A wise and Christ-
honoring husband will not take advantage of his leadership role,
and a wise and Christ-honoring wife will not try to undermine
her husband's leadership. Either approach causes disunity and
friction in marriage. For the wife, submission means willingly
following her husband's leadership in Christ. For the husband,
it means putting aside his own interests in order to care for his
wife. Submission is rarely a problem in homes where both partners have a strong relationship with Christ and where each is
concerned for the happiness of the other.

IT TAKES BOTH
Having established the principle of Spirit-led submission as an
obligation for all Christians, Paul next illustrated how this principle
was to be lived out in the home. He called upon wives to submit
to their husbands as to the Lord. This should not be taken to
mean that wives are to be doormats, allowing their husband to
walk over them; nor are they to be silent partners, wordlessly
carrying out their husband's directives. It means that wives are
to willingly support their husband's leadership—not balking or
undermining him. They are to be active participants in the
challenging task of running a Christian home. They are to do
everything they can to encourage and support their husbands'
leadership in the home, but not blindly or unquestioningly. When
the husband is in error or even in outright sin, it is the wife's
responsibility to lovingly confront him, pointing him back to the
lordship of Christ as the ultimate authority. It takes both partners
to make a Christian marriage and home.

5:25-26 **Husbands, love your wives, just as Christ loved the church and
gave himself up for her, in order to make her holy by cleansing
her with the washing of water by the word.**NRSV Paul also had
words for husbands—to *love* their wives. Why did Paul tell wives

to "submit" and husbands to "love"? Perhaps Christian women, newly freed in Christ, found submission difficult; perhaps Christian men, used to the Roman custom of giving unlimited power to the head of the family, were not used to treating their wives with sacrificial respect and love. Of course, both husbands and wives should submit to each other (5:21) just as both should love each other. Thus, "submission" reaffirms the new covenant of equality as well as the affirmation of marriage in which the partners voluntarily and joyously submit in order to seek each other's best.

Some Christians have thought that Paul was negative about marriage because of his counsel in 1 Corinthians 7:32-38. These verses in Ephesians, however, show a high view of marriage. Here marriage is not a practical necessity or a cure for lust but a picture of the relationship between Christ and his church! Husbands are called to love their wives *just as Christ loved the church and gave himself up for her.* That Christ "gave himself" indicates a sacrificial, substitutionary surrendering of himself to death. Christ sacrificed himself for the church because of his love for it. Husbands, then, should be ready to make whatever sacrifices are necessary for their wives. Marriage is a holy union, a living symbol, a precious relationship that needs tender, self-sacrificing care. How should a man love his wife? (1) He should be willing to sacrifice everything for her. (2) He should make her well-being of primary importance. (3) He should care for her as he cares for his own body. No wife needs to fear submitting to a man who treats her in this way.

Paul further explained that Christ gave himself up for the church *in order to make her holy by cleansing her with the washing of water by the word.* Christ's death sanctifies and cleanses the church. He cleanses his people from the old ways of sin and sets them apart for his special sacred service. Christ cleansed the church by the "washing of water." This most likely refers to baptism, but this is only a metaphor, for baptism is a picture of the cleansing that has occurred because of Christ's sacrificial death. Through baptism we are prepared for entrance into the church just as ancient Near Eastern brides were prepared for marriage by a ceremonial bath. It is God's Word that cleanses us (John 17:17; Titus 3:5).

The phrase "by the word" has four possible meanings: (1) the words spoken by the new believer confessing his or her faith in Christ; (2) the marriage vows where Christian faith is pledged and the promise of love is made; (3) the confession at baptism where words of the Bible are repeated by the baptizer and the believer; (4) the gospel message—being made clean by believing

in God's Word given in the gospel message. Most likely it refers
to the third meaning and is closely associated with baptism.

How does this apply to marriage? Probably the details need not
be carried too far; Paul was quoting a hymn and did not mean for
each detail to correspond to the marriage relationship. But this does
paint the picture of mutual sanctification and self-sacrifice. Indeed,
Paul had that thought in mind when he wrote in 1 Corinthians
7:12-16 that the unbelieving partner may be drawn to God by the
believing partner. Paul was telling husbands to draw their wives
closer to Christ and be a part of his sanctifying process. Peter applied
the same thought to wives: "Wives, in the same way, accept the
authority of your husbands, so that, even if some of them do not
obey the word, they may be won over without a word by their
wives' conduct, when they see the purity and reverence of your
lives" (1 Peter 3:1-2 NRSV).

HONORED ROLES
Next Paul turned to the husband's role in the care and mainte-
nance of the Christian home. That role is nothing less than overwhelming: to love their wives as Christ loved his church. If the
task of submitting to male headship seems burdensome to wives,
the obligation to love as Christ did will seem out of reach to
husbands. How are men to do that? The same way Christ loves
the church: sacrificially, compassionately, gently, and lovingly.
Jesus laid down his life for the church; husbands are called to
give themselves unreservedly for their wives and children. John
Stott summed it up well when he wrote of Jesus, "His headship
expresses care rather than control, responsibility rather than rule."
Healthy, Spirit-led relationships are not concerned with power,
with who's in control. They are concerned with Christlikeness,
with honoring him in their relationship with one another.

**5:27 So as to present the church to himself in splendor, without a
spot or wrinkle or anything of the kind—yes, so that she may
be holy and without blemish.**NRSV Continuing from 5:26, probably
as part of an early Christian hymn, this verse explains why Christ
gave himself up for the church in order to make the church holy—
so as to present the church to himself in splendor. The "presentation" pictures a future wedding; this is like the betrothal period,
which for the Jews was as binding as marriage. The church age is
the interim before the "wedding" when the church will at last be
presented to Christ as his "bride" (Revelation 19:7). During this
time, the church is making itself ready, as a bride would be preparing for her wedding. The "splendor" may refer to the shared glory
of the church as it progresses toward Christlike perfection. This

may also be an allusion to the "riches" that Christ bestows on his church, as referred to earlier in this letter (1:7, 18; 2:7; 3:8, 16).

The phrase "without a spot or wrinkle or anything of the kind . . . holy and without blemish" again pictures the bride's preparations in order to be ready. It was traditional for a bride to take a ritual bath just before her wedding as a symbol of her chastity. Similarly, the sacrament of baptism demonstrates the Christian's desire that God should find him or her pure and faithful when Christ returns to claim his bride, the church. The church does not make itself holy and blameless; instead, it has already been made so through the blood of Christ. But the church should be growing toward Christlikeness as it awaits the arrival of Christ at his second coming. Moral and spiritual uprightness should be the qualities of Christ's church.

5:28 In the same way, husbands should love their wives as they do their own bodies. He who loves his wife loves himself.NRSV *In the same way* means that there exists between the husband and the wife the same union as between Christ and the church. Following from 5:27, husbands should be as concerned for their wife's spiritual growth and closeness to the Lord as Christ is for the church. Paul expressed this unity in physical terms, for the husband and wife become "one flesh" through marriage (Genesis 2:24; see 5:31 below, where Paul quoted this verse). So Christ and his church become "one" through spiritual union (see 4:4). As such, the church is Christ's body: "Now you are the body of Christ, and each one of you is a part of it" (1 Corinthians 12:27 NIV). Christ "gave himself" for the church (5:25), so *husbands should love their wives as they do their own bodies.* The spiritual and physical union between a husband and wife is as total and complete as the union a person has with his or her own body. When a man loves his wife, he *loves himself,* for she is so much a part of him. The words "loves himself" probably look back to the words of Jesus to "love your neighbor as yourself" (Matthew 22:39). This is a beautiful picture of the mutuality that should be a part of every marriage. This picture shattered the cultural norms of the day, in which a wife was often considered no more than "property." No, Paul says, in fact, the relationship is so deep and intimate that the husband and wife are a single being. The husband loves his wife not as an extension of self-love but because it is advantageous both to her and to himself. The Greek word for "love" is *agapao,* referring to that giving love that seeks the highest good for the other. When a husband loves his wife with this kind of love, they both will benefit. A wife need not worry about submitting to a husband who treats her this way.

5:29-30 For no one ever hates his own body, but he nourishes and tenderly cares for it, just as Christ does for the church, because we are members of his body.NRSV The fact that *no one ever hates his own body* refers not to self-centeredness but to self-preservation, the natural self-concern that causes people to feed and care for themselves. As a man *nourishes and tenderly cares for* his own body, he should also do the same for his wife, who is one with him. Why? Again Paul draws on of the example given by Christ, who nourishes and cares for his body, *the church.* As Christ nourishes and cares for believers, so husbands must imitate Christ in their loving concern and care for their wives. But more than just an example, Christ provides the basis for the husband's loving attention to his wife's needs. For the husband, and indeed every believer, receives this loving attention from Christ *because we are members of his body.* He cherishes and nourishes us as living parts of his body. (See John 15:1-8, where Jesus used the analogy of the vine and the branches to teach this concept.) The union of husband and wife reflects the union of the body of Christ; Christ is the life of both relationships (1:22-23; 4:12, 16).

CHRISTIAN RELATIONSHIPS

A Christian Husband and Father	*A Christian Wife and Mother*
Remains faithful to his wife in a lifelong commitment to her (1 Corinthians 7:10-11)	Remains faithful to her husband in a lifelong commitment to him (1 Corinthians 7:10-11)
Meets his wife's sexual needs (1 Corinthians 7:3-5)	Meets her husband's sexual needs (1 Corinthians 7:3-5)
Loves his wife as much as he loves himself (Ephesians 5:25-30)	Submits to her husband's leadership role in the home (Ephesians 5:22, 24; Colossians 3:18; 1 Peter 3:1)
Joins with his wife in complete unity (Ephesians 5:31)	Respects her husband (Ephesians 5:33)
Brings up his children in the training and instruction of the Lord (Ephesians 6:4)	Develops inward charm and beauty (1 Peter 3:3-5)
Treats his wife kindly (Colossians 3:19)	
Provides for the material needs of his family (1 Timothy 5:8)	
Treats his wife with consideration and respect (1 Peter 3:7)	

5:31 "For this reason a man shall leave his father and mother and be joined to his wife, and the two shall become one flesh."^{NKJV} The creation story tells of God's plan for husband and wife to be one (Genesis 2:24); Jesus also referred to this plan (Matthew 19:4-6). The union of husband and wife merges two persons in such a way that little can affect one without also affecting the other. Oneness in marriage does not mean one person's losing his or her personality in the personality of the other. Instead, it means that each person cares for the other as though caring for himself or herself, learning to anticipate the other's needs, helping the other person reach his or her potential.

This verse refers to spiritual marriage as represented by natural marriage, in which Christ leaves his Father to seek his own love, the church. In a natural marriage, the husband and wife complement one another. So Christ and the church must function together; Christ needed the church in order to assume his position as its Head. Christ is the Head of the church as the husband is the head of the wife (Romans 6:5; 1 Corinthians 11:3). Christ and his church are indissolubly joined (Matthew 19:6; John 10:28-29).

5:32 This is a great mystery, and I am applying it to Christ and the church.^{NRSV} The union of husband and wife, although sometimes imperfect, provides the best picture to describe the union of Christ with his church. The picture we experience in marriage is an analogy of the relationship of Christ and believers. The words in Genesis take on a more profound meaning as we contemplate Christ and his church. "This is a great mystery" might better be translated, "There is a profound truth hidden here." As Paul contemplated the mutual love and loyalty, loving headship of the husband and loving submission of the wife, riches bestowed, intimacy and oneness, and self-sacrifice that should describe every marriage, he saw in these a picture of *Christ and the church.*

5:33 Each of you, however, should love his wife as himself, and a wife should respect her husband.^{NRSV} This verse returns to the commands about human marriage, summarizing the attitudes that are to be shown by both husband and wife. Here Paul addressed husbands first. *Each of you,* he said, *should love his wife as himself.* This is the core of Christian marriage. Each wife, in turn, *should respect her husband.* How many marriages could be made healthy and strong if both husband and wife would fulfill these simple yet profound instructions? Where husband and wife love and respect each other, they have both a healthy marriage and a healthy family life in which to bring up children. The relationships of children and parents are covered in the next chapter.

Ephesians 6

If our faith in Christ is real, it will usually prove itself at home, in our relationships with those who know us best. Children and parents have a responsibility to each other. The fact that Paul took the time to directly address those who were regarded by some as the "lower" and "less important" members of society (wives, children, and slaves) shows that he raised them to a level of importance and responsibility in the body of Christ. All Christians are to be responsible in their positions, living as Christ would have them live.

6:1 Children, obey your parents in the Lord, for this is right.[NKJV] Continuing the theme of Christian submission, Paul turned next to children. He assumed that children would be in the congregation of believers as this letter was read. By even addressing them—a segment of society that was considered to be virtually without rights—Paul elevated them and invested them with dignity and worth unheard of in the Roman world at the time. His command to them is simple: *Obey your parents in the Lord.* This is not an absolute command; when a parent tells a child to do something unbiblical, immoral, or unethical, the law of God supersedes the will of the parent. But aside from those extremes, children are to obey their mothers and fathers. This is the way God intends it. It's easy to see the immediate practical benefits of this for both children and parents because parents usually really do know best.

The Greek word for *children (tekna)* refers to young children living at home (see also Colossians 3:20, where the same word is used). The word "obey" conveys a stronger demand than the submission required of wives (5:22). God requires children to obey because children need to rely on the wisdom of their parents. Jesus himself submitted to the authority of his earthly parents, despite his authority as the Messiah (Luke 2:51). All young children will, at times, disobey and test their parents' limits. As they get older, they will understand why God wants them to obey. Obedience that recognizes parents' authority can carry over into recognizing God's authority. God's plan for his people includes solid family relationships where there exists respect, obedience, submission, and love for one another. When both parents and children love God, all of them will seek to obey and please him.

PARENTS AND CHILDREN
The parent-child relationship is the arena in which the child is to learn to submit to and respect his elders and those in authority over him—including God. Do you require your children to obey you? Do you help other parents by setting a good example for them in this area? Don't be misled or dissuaded by the media or our permissive culture. Let the Bible be the voice of wisdom that cuts through the noise of our society. If you love your children, teach them the value and blessings of obedience.

6:2-3 **"Honor your father and mother," which is the first commandment with promise: "that it may be well with you and you may live long on the earth."**NKJV Paul added the authority of the revealed law to the natural law described in 6:1, quoting the fifth commandment, recorded in Exodus 20:12, *Honor your father and mother.* Obeying and honoring are different. To obey means to do what another says to do; to honor means to respect and love. Children are to obey while under their parents' care, but they must honor their parents for life. Paul described this as *the first commandment with promise,* that of prolonged life, which he quoted in the remainder of the verse. How is this the first commandment with a promise? It is neither the first commandment, nor the first with a promise, since the second commandment carries a promise with it. Commentators offer many explanations. Two are most helpful: (1) This is the first commandment (after the first four, which are general commandments) that deals with social involvements and codes for behavior. (2) More likely, this is the first or primary commandment for children to follow, but it holds a promise applicable to them.

HONOR
Paul instructed children not only to obey their parents but to honor them as well. It is entirely possible to obey without honor—who hasn't seen a child do what he or she is told, but with clenched fists and teeth and an "I'm only doing this because you're making me" attitude? To honor is to go beyond obedience. It is to show respect and esteem for someone and to treat him or her with dignity. Children do not always agree with their parents (and that holds true for children of all ages), but they can always treat them with respect. It is incumbent upon parents to teach this to their children and to make it easier for them to do so by acting in respectable, honorable ways.

CHILDREN AND THEIR PARENTS

The Scriptures have much to say about how children should treat their parents.

Who said it	Where it's said	Do	Don't
Moses in the Law	Exodus 20:12; Deuteronomy 5:16	Honor and respect them	
	Exodus 21:15		Attack them
	Exodus 21:17; Leviticus 20:9		Curse them
	Deuteronomy 21:18-21	Obey them	Rebel against them
Solomon in the Proverbs	Proverbs 23:22	Listen to them	
	Proverbs 28:24		Rob them
	Proverbs 30:11		Curse them
	Proverbs 30:17		Mock them
Jesus in the Gospels	Matthew 15:4-6; Mark 7:10-13	Honor and provide for them	Curse and neglect them
	Matthew 19:19	Honor them	
	Mark 10:19	Honor them	
	Luke 14:26		Honor them above God
Paul in the Epistles	Ephesians 6:1	Obey them	
	Ephesians 6:2	Honor them	

The promise should not be the main motive for honoring parents; rather, the main motive should be to do God's will, and the promise that accompanies the command indicates this. Paul adapted the promise recorded in Exodus 20:12 and Deuteronomy 5:16. As children obey the command to honor their parents, they show an attitude of love and respect that they carry over into their relationship with God. Such an attitude provides a community that helps provide for and protect the aged. On the individual level, as each person cares for older people, the elderly live longer, and the younger people help pass the values down to the next generation.

The word "honor" also refers to the attitude of slaves toward masters (1 Timothy 6:1), of husbands toward wives (1 Peter 3:7), and general attitude toward others, especially those in leadership (Romans 13:7). Jesus made this an unconditional demand (Mark 7:10-13). Some societies honor their elders. They respect their wisdom, defer to their authority, and pay attention to their comfort and happiness. Christians should act this way. Where elders are respected, long life becomes a blessing, not a burden to them. Paul instructed the church to be a community that cares for older people. This will be especially important as people in North America age. By the year 2021, one in six people will be over sixty-five years of age. Honoring our aging parents will be crucial as our Christian duty.

6:4 And, fathers, do not provoke your children to anger, but bring them up in the discipline and instruction of the Lord.[NRSV] Parental discipline should help children learn, not exasperate and *provoke* them *to anger.* In Colossians 3:21, Paul gave the same advice, adding that if children are disciplined in unloving and irresponsible ways, they may become discouraged and resentful. In families of Paul's day, the father had full legal rights over his children and often ran his household with rigid control. In Jewish families, the fathers were responsible for the education of the children. Paul did not have to establish the fathers' authority; rather, his aim was to set the limits on harsh treatment. Parenting is not easy—it takes lots of patience to raise children in a loving, Christ-honoring manner. But frustration and anger should not be causes for discipline. Parents can remove the exasperating effect of their discipline by avoiding nagging, labeling, criticizing, or dominating. Don't goad your children into resenting you. Paul wrote specifically to *fathers* because, in that culture, fathers were the absolute head of the home, with complete control and authority. For Paul to say that they needed to treat their children as human beings and consider their feelings was revolutionary. As Christ changed the way husbands and wives related, so he changed the way parents and children related.

THE BALANCE
As he did with his instructions to husbands and wives, Paul now struck a balance with his advice to children by addressing their parents, especially fathers. Fathers (and mothers) are to teach their children to honor and obey, yes, but they are to do so in a way that does not "provoke [their] children to anger." We may remember what it feels like to be exasperated or angered by an unreasonable or even cruel or abusive parent or parent figure. Paul warns parents not to do that to their own children. Teach them obedience and respect, yes, but do it in such a way as not to drive them to rage or despair. Martin Luther, whose own father was very strict, once wrote: "Spare the rod and spoil the child—that is true. But beside the rod keep an apple to give him when he has done well." Check yourself: Do you try to encourage and praise at least as often as you scold or correct?

Parents ought not provoke their children, and neither should they abandon their responsibility to guide, correct, and discipline them. Parents still have a job to do for their children—to *bring them up in the discipline and instruction of the Lord.* The words "bring up" imply nourishing and cherishing. "Discipline" includes punishment for wrongdoing combined with persistent love (see Proverbs 13:24; 22:6, 15; 23:14), all as part of the *instruction* of a child. We must explain appropriate behavior to our children, correct them as they disobey, and encourage them when they obey. Both discipline and instruction are focused in "the Lord," for God-fearing parents desire God-fearing children. Thus, discipline and instruction are given in the context of the parents' relationship with the Lord, as described in the Old Testament:

■ *Love the* LORD *your God with all your heart and with all your soul and with all your strength. These commandments that I give you today are to be upon your hearts. Impress them on your children. Talk about them when you sit at home and when you walk along the road, when you lie down and when you get up. Tie them as symbols on your hands and bind them on your foreheads. Write them on the doorframes of your houses and on your gates. (Deuteronomy 6:5-9* NIV*)*

Discipline and instruction in the Lord form the foundation for bringing up children.

TEACH
After the negative command ("Do not provoke your children to anger"), Paul adds an affirmative one: "Bring them up in the discipline and instruction of the Lord." We must also be diligent to give them the instruction and encouragement so vital to their upbringing. William Hendrickson put it this way: "The heart of Christian nurture is to bring the heart of the child to the heart of his Savior." Do you read the Bible to your children? Do you tell them the great stories of the heroic men and women of the faith who've gone before? Do you pray for and with them daily? Do you take them to worship and Christian education classes, and let them see how important your involvement in the church is to you? Can they see the difference Christ makes in your life?

SLAVES AND MASTERS / 6:5-9

Slaves played a significant part in this society as well as in most societies of that day. No ancient government ever considered abolishing slavery as it was such an instrumental part of the

Mediterranean economy. There were several million of them in the Roman Empire at this time. People could become slaves by being born to a woman who was a slave, by being made a slave as punishment for a crime, by being kidnapped from another land, and by being conquered by another nation (slave dealers would buy captured prisoners and send them to the slave markets to be sold for a profit). Sometimes, however, parents would sell their children into slavery. And some would voluntarily become slaves in order to pay a debt. Usually those with financial means owned slaves. How slave owners treated their slaves could vary greatly, depending on the temperament of the owner and the performance of the slave. Slave owners had absolute power over their slaves. However, not all slaves were badly treated. Many became like members of the family in which they served—some caring for and practically raising the owner's children. Some slaves could own property, have their own slaves, and even obtain other employment. Under Roman law, a slave could often expect to be set free as a reward for hard work.

Because many slaves and owners had become Christians, the early church had to deal straightforwardly with the question of master/slave relations. Masters and slaves had to learn how to live together in Christian households. They were to be treated equally in the church. In Paul's day, women, children, and slaves had few rights. In the church, however, they had freedoms that society denied them.

6:5 Slaves, obey your earthly masters with deep respect and fear. Serve them sincerely as you would serve Christ.^{NLT} Paul used the same word for "obey" here that he used in 6:1 for children obeying their parents. Slaves were to obey the commands and desires of their masters; this was their duty because of the authority of the master. Paul addressed the slaves who had become Christians and needed to understand how their new faith affected their service to human masters. Paul advised the slaves to treat their *earthly masters with deep respect and fear* (referring to an attitude of reverence and honor, a desire to do right). These slaves had been set free from slavery to sin, but they were not freed from serving their masters. The word "earthly" distinguishes these slave owners from the ultimate Master, God himself. Paul explained that God wanted the slaves to fulfill their responsibilities in this world as if they were serving Christ. Even more than that, the slaves were actually rendering obedience to Christ when they obeyed their masters. Such service should be accomplished *sincerely,* meaning without pretense or evil motivation.

Paul neither condemned nor condoned slavery in these

words. On one hand, Paul was not interested in starting a
revolutionary movement to attempt to destroy the sanctions
of the Roman Empire. On the other hand, Paul *was* starting a
revolutionary movement although he was not a political orga-
nizer. Paul's revolutionary zeal was developed in the context
of the church, where selflessness and love constituted new
relationships based not on power but on mutual affirmation.
(See also 1 Corinthians 7:20-24; Colossians 3:22–4:1.)

**6:6 Work hard, but not just to please your masters when they are
watching. As slaves of Christ, do the will of God with all your
heart.**ᴺᴸᵀ Slaves were to *work hard* for their masters, not only when
they were being watched and hoping for a reward, but at all times.
They should work not only for human approval but also to *do the
will of God* with all their hearts. Why? Because they were *slaves of
Christ* as well as of human masters. They should work hard to do
their job well in this world, while at the same time working hard for
Christ as they look forward to the next world, where all believers
will serve Christ in his kingdom. All believers, as slaves of Christ
(whether slaves or free in this world) should do the *will of God*
with all their hearts. To do something *with all your heart* means to
act wholeheartedly, not halfheartedly, doing your work well enough
to pass God's inspection.

JOB OPPORTUNITIES
Paul's instructions encourage responsibility and integrity on the
job. Christian employees should do their jobs as if Jesus Christ
were their supervisor, and Christian employers should treat
their employees fairly and with respect. Can you be trusted to
do your best, even when the boss is not around? Do you work
hard and with enthusiasm? Do you treat your employees as
people, not machines? Remember that no matter whom you
work for and no matter who works for you, the One you
ultimately should want to please is your Father in heaven.

**6:7-8 Render service with enthusiasm, as to the Lord and not to
men and women, knowing that whatever good we do, we
will receive the same again from the Lord, whether we are
slaves or free.**ᴺᴿˢⱽ Slaves had a variety of tasks—running
errands, caring for or teaching children, cleaning, preparing
meals, or doing menial work. Paul gave their jobs a new dignity,
telling these slaves to *render service with enthusiasm, as to the
Lord and not to men and women.* Our true Master, the Lord
Jesus, knows the state of our hearts and knows if we are shirk-
ing the job that we, as his slaves, have been given to do. We

should also faithfully serve our earthly masters in this way.
The Christian slave should obey as an expression of his or her
commitment to the Lord.

Slaves had little opportunity to get out of slavery, and they
received little, if any, monetary compensation for their work. Yet
in their work, they could do *good,* and in so doing, they would
receive the same again from the Lord along with their free brothers
and sisters.

HOLY WORK
Paul here addressed another group that had virtually no rights
and was often held in rather low esteem: slaves. He told them
to "render service with enthusiasm, as to the Lord." This difficult
instruction has two implications we would do well to remember:
(1) Our work needs to be worth offering to the Lord, whatever
our field. How shameful for Christian employees to do their
work in a substandard, slipshod, or unethical manner. Those
people lose all credibility with their coworkers. (2) Our work can
be a holy offering to God. Our attitude of service transforms our
menial tasks into beautiful sacrifices of love.

Do these truths cause you to rethink the way you do your
job? Are there areas of your job performance for which you
need to repent and possibly even apologize or make restitution
to someone? Your work can be holy. Remember to do it in a
way that honors God.

**6:9 And masters, treat your slaves in the same way. Do not
threaten them, since you know that he who is both their
Master and yours is in heaven, and there is no favoritism
with him.**NIV Paul also had words for the *masters,* for those who
had become Christians needed guidance in relationships with
their Christian slaves. Paul advised them to treat their slaves *in
the same way.* In other words, the masters should have the same
concern for God's will and for the slaves' well-being as the slaves
were expected to show toward God and their masters.

In those days, slaves may have been conquered peoples from
foreign lands or people sold into slavery to recover debts. It was
difficult for a slave to rise from that social caste. Often slaves
were treated as less than human, thus Paul's advice to masters,
Do not threaten them. Without attempting to overturn the social
structure of a worldwide empire, Paul applied Christ's inward
transforming principles to the system. Paul did not advise the
Christian masters to free their slaves; in fact, in some cases,
setting them free might not have been the best action. Instead,
Paul told the masters to remember *that he who is both their
Master and yours is in heaven.* Although Christians may be at

different levels in earthly society, we are all equal before God. He
does not show *favoritism;* no one is more important than anyone
else. Paul's letter to Philemon stresses the same point: Philemon,
the master, and Onesimus, his slave, had become brothers in
Christ.

MASTERS
Suppose you are a supervisor or manager and you find that
one of your subordinates made a major mistake. You are just
about to deliver a very severe reprimand when a friend comes
alongside and says, "Careful—that's the boss's daughter."
Would that change the way you would treat her? Paul says
something similar to Christian masters of slaves. Don't threaten
them, he says; you both have the same heavenly Master. Treat
them with respect and dignity as befits any child of God. This
was revolutionary advice in its time and social context. The
principle still applies today to employers and employees.
Employers are not to treat their workers in a demeaning or
unnecessarily harsh manner but as persons created in the
image of God. If you are a boss or owner, do you treat your
subordinates the way you want to be treated? Keep in mind
that you will answer one day to *your* heavenly Master.

WEARING THE WHOLE ARMOR OF GOD / 6:10-20

In the Christian life, we battle against rulers and authorities (the
powerful evil forces of fallen angels headed by Satan, who is a
vicious fighter, see 1 Peter 5:8). To withstand their attacks, we
must depend on God's strength and use every piece of his armor.
Paul was not only giving this counsel to the church, the body of
Christ, but to all individuals within the church. The whole body
needs to be armed. As you battle against "the powers of this dark
world," fight in the strength of the church, whose power comes
from the Holy Spirit. What can your church do to be a Christian
armory?

6:10 Finally, be strong in the Lord and in his mighty power.[NIV]
The word "finally" signals the beginning of Paul's conclusion
to his letter, where he will give words of vital importance for
his readers. In this letter, Paul explained the need for unity in
the body of believers; here he further explained the need for
that unity—there will be inevitable clashes with evil, and the
church must be ready to stand and fight.

"Be strong in the Lord" refers to strength derived from God,
not strength we humans have to somehow obtain. The words
"be strong" describe continual empowering of the Christian

community. God's strength and *his mighty power* are part of the
kingdom blessings available to God's people. At the beginning
of this letter, Paul prayed for believers to know God's "incomparably great power for us who believe. That power is like the
working of his mighty strength, which he exerted in Christ when
he raised him from the dead and seated him at his right hand
in the heavenly realms" (1:19-20 NIV). The power that raised
Christ from the dead empowers God's people as they prepare
for the spiritual battle they must face on this earth. They will
need it, for, as the text continues, the struggle occurs in the spiritual realm and must be won with spiritual weapons. While the
victory is certain, the battle still must be waged. Paul's words
are all in the plural, addressed to the church, who, like a warrior, needs to put on the complete armor of God. Of course, this
combined effort calls for each member's fullest participation.

TRAINING

If you want to complete a marathon, you have to run hundreds of
training miles. If you want to learn a foreign language, you have
to spend some hours memorizing declensions and conjugations.
If you want to play the piano, you have to learn the scales and
how to read music. And if you want to accomplish anything for
God, you have to spend time with the spiritual disciplines: Bible
study, prayer, church involvement, fasting, serving. Being a
Christian is not a learned skill or discipline; it's a living relationship
with our living Lord Jesus. But like any other relationship, if you
want it to be deep and meaningful—beyond the superficial and
empty formalities—it takes time and commitment. Do you set
aside time for spiritual training?

**6:11 Put on the whole armor of God, so that you may be able to
stand against the wiles of the devil.**^{NRSV} God empowers his
people, but he does not send them into battle unarmed. God's
people must *put on the whole armor of God* (see also Romans
13:12). The *panoplia,* or full armor, means complete equipment,
head-to-toe protection, both defensively and offensively. This
gear was for hand-to-hand combat, not for appearances. This
"armor of God" was mentioned in the Old Testament. Isaiah
59:17 describes God as wearing the breastplate of righteousness and the helmet of salvation. Paul wrote this letter while
chained to a Roman soldier. Certainly the soldier's armor must
have brought this metaphor to mind. Paul described a divine
and complete "outfit" that God gives believers in order to
provide all we need to *be able to stand against the wiles of*

the devil. The devil rules the world of darkness, the kingdom opposed to God. "Stand against" was a military term meaning to resist the enemy, hold the position, and offer no surrender. (For more on "stand," see 6:13-14; 1 Corinthians 16:13; Colossians 4:12; James 4:7; 1 Peter 5:8-9.) Also called Satan, the devil will not fight fair; his "wiles" will often include subtle tricks and schemes. Our "ability to stand" in battle depends on our use of "the whole armor of God."

ARMED AND READY
Why would Christians not want to use the full armor? What keeps them from using God's power?
1. They don't sense danger or recognize the power of the enemy.
2. They don't have all the weapons. They have never been taught the significance and importance of those weapons.
3. They are untrained in the use of those weapons. Without practice, no soldier can be ready for battle.
4. They may be in a comfort zone. Perhaps they are nowhere near the battle or they are somehow compromising with the enemy.
If you are a church leader, make sure your church prepares people. All believers must take hold of the power that God has made available to them. They cannot fight the battle without it.

6:12 For our struggle is not against enemies of blood and flesh, but against the rulers, against the authorities, against the cosmic powers of this present darkness, against the spiritual forces of evil in the heavenly places.[NRSV] The Christians face a *struggle* against evil—describing hand-to-hand combat. But we are not in an earthly military campaign—our battle *is not against enemies of blood and flesh.* Instead, we battle the demons over whom Satan has control. Demons work to tempt people to sin. They were not created by Satan because God is the Creator of all. Rather, the demons are fallen angels who joined Satan in his rebellion and thus became perverted and evil. The descriptive words "rulers," "authorities," "cosmic powers," and "spiritual forces of evil in the heavenly places" reveal the characteristics of these enemies as well as their sphere of operations. "Rulers and authorities" are cosmic powers, or demons, mentioned in 1:21. These spiritual beings have limited power. "Cosmic powers of this present darkness" refers to those spiritual powers who aspire to world control. The "spiritual

> In the New Testament it is not believers who tremble at the power of Satan, but demons who tremble at the power of God.
> *Stephen Travis*

forces of evil in the heavenly places" refers to the demons' dwelling, planets and stars, from which the demons control the lives of people. Paul used the names of groups of evil powers not so much to establish classes or distinguish demonic powers as to show the full extent of Satan's warfare.

Here is a host of spiritual forces arrayed against us, requiring us to use God's full armor. These are real and powerful beings, not mere fantasies. Believers must not underestimate them. The Ephesians had practiced magic and witchcraft (Acts 19:19), so they were well aware of the power of the darkness. As the Bible explains the kingdom of light, the kingdom of darkness is exposed. These powers are "cosmic" and "spiritual"; thus, we fight the battle in that realm. (For discussion on "in the heavenly places," see 1:3, 20; 2:6; 3:10.)

We face a powerful army whose goal is to defeat Christ's church. When we believe in Christ, the satanic beings become our enemies, and they try every device to turn us away from him and back to sin. Although believers are assured of victory, we must engage in the struggle until Christ returns because Satan constantly battles against all who are on God's side. Although Satan and his demons rule the world, they do not rule the universe; the stolen kingdom will be regained by Christ, the rightful ruler, when he appears. In the meantime, believers need supernatural power to defeat Satan, and God has provided this power by giving us his Holy Spirit within us and his armor surrounding us. (See also 1 Timothy 1:18; 6:12.)

KNOW THE ENEMY

We fight a spiritual battle, but we might well ask, who is the enemy? It's not the nonbeliever, although occasionally you will meet a person so full of evil and rebellion against God that he or she actually declares himself or herself the enemy of Christianity. The secular media or world systems work relentlessly to undermine God's truth, but they are not the enemy either, although they are often tools in his hands. Our enemy is Satan and the spiritual "forces of evil." Satan, the deceiver (Genesis 3), the accuser (Zechariah 3), the destroyer (1 Peter 5), is the adversary of our souls and of the souls of our friends and loved ones. As Paul sounded this battle call, he wanted us to know whom we're fighting. Our enemy is powerful, but he is also a defeated foe. As you prepare to engage him in spiritual warfare, don't be intimidated by his influence. Use the full armor of God and stand together with other believers.

6:13 Therefore take up the whole armor of God, that you may be able to withstand in the evil day, and having done all, to

stand.NKJV *Therefore,* the believers' response to the reality of this warfare should be to *take up the whole armor of God.* The armor is ready for us; we merely need to *take* it. This changes the clothing metaphor slightly from 4:24, where Paul had instructed the believers to "put on" the new self. "Take up" is a technical military term describing preparation for battle. The armor is available, but the believer-soldier must "take it up" in order to be ready. We would be neglectful to do otherwise, for the battle is real, and we are Satan's targets. Only with the armor will believers be able to *withstand,* a word describing standing against great opposition; indeed, it would be impossible to stand on our strength alone. Christian soldiers must be able to hold their ground and not flee or surrender under Satan's attacks. *The evil day* refers to the hours of trial that have within themselves the seeds of the last and greatest trial. Christians must be prepared for every day's conflicts with the forces of evil.

The words "having done all, to stand" probably summarize the believers' victory after the battle. In ancient times, those still standing after the battle were the victors. The whole context implies that we have the victory. We must participate in Christ's victory over Satan. We know the outcome of the war, but individual battles can be lost if any believers have not *done all* in order *to stand* (see also James 4:7; 1 Peter 5:9).

6:14 Stand therefore, and fasten the belt of truth around your waist.NRSV In order to *stand therefore* in the heat of battle, believers need every piece of God's armor. The order of the pieces listed in the following verses is the order in which a soldier would put them on. First, Paul wrote, *fasten the belt of truth around your waist.* This belt, also called a girdle, was about six inches wide. Probably made of leather, it held together the clothing underneath as well as holding the other pieces of armor in place, such as the breastplate and the sheath for the sword. It may have contained a "breech-clout," an apron that protected the lower abdomen. It may have also braced the back in order to give strength. When the belt was fastened, the soldier was "on duty," ready to fight. A slackened belt meant "off duty." Christians, however, must face each day with a fastened belt, ready to fight the battle when needed.

As the belt formed the foundation of the soldier's armor, the truth is the foundation of the Christian life. This "truth" refers to the believer's character as a person who can be relied on for the truth. It certainly also refers to the truth of God's Word and his message in the gospel. If we could not be absolutely sure of our faith, if we were not sure that Jesus is "the truth" (John 14:6), then there would be little use for the armor or in attempting to fight any battle. God's truth, as revealed to us through Jesus Christ, forms the foundation of victorious Christian living.

When the enemy, the father of lies (John 8:44), attacks with his lies, half-truths, and distortions, we believers can stand on the truth we believe. Jesus prayed for his followers: "Sanctify them by Your truth. Your word is truth" (John 17:17 NKJV).

And put on the breastplate of righteousness.NRSV Next, the soldier must *put on the breastplate of righteousness.* A breastplate was a large leather, bronze, or chain-mail piece that protected the body from the neck to the thighs. In Isaiah 59:17, God "put on righteousness as his breastplate." Protecting the vital organs, the breastplate was a vital piece in the soldier's armor. No soldier would go into battle without his breastplate. Often this had a back piece too, protecting the body from hits from behind.

"Righteousness" provides a significant defense; it gives the evidence that we have been made right with God and that this righteousness has been given us by the Holy Spirit. Believers have been made righteous through the blood of Christ. The believers then want to live in uprightness and integrity, desiring to please the One who saved them. Yet that won't be easy. Satan is ready for battle at every turn, willing to hit us unfairly from behind if given the chance. Righteousness is the opposite of Satan's complete wickedness. Satan seeks to thwart righteous living.

When the enemy, the accuser (Revelation 12:10), tries to convince us that we are not really saved, that we just keep on disappointing God, and that we're "poor excuses" for Christians, we can stand up to him because of the righteousness we have been promised through our faith in Jesus Christ. "This righteousness from God comes through faith in Jesus Christ to all who believe" (Romans 3:22 NIV).

BATTLE STATIONS
Suppose you were in a fight to the death with someone and you held a sword in your hands. In the middle of the conflict, your opponent says, "Hey, you call that puny thing a sword? It doesn't look like much of a sword to me. In fact, I don't think it's a sword at all." Would you drop your weapon and try to fight without it? Of course not. Yet often we Christians surrender our weapons to a skeptical world. In 6:14-17 Paul describes our weaponry: the belt of truth, breastplate of righteousness, footwear of the gospel, shield of faith, helmet of salvation, and the sword of the Spirit—the Word of God. That is an impressive display of armament, regardless of who believes it. As you engage in spiritual combat, make sure you have and use all the weapons God makes available.

6:15 And with your feet fitted with the readiness that comes from the gospel of peace.NIV A soldier wore special sandals or military shoes that protected his feet without slowing him down. Roman soldiers had special shoes made of soft leather with studded soles. This allowed them to march farther and faster as well as giving them facility of motion in battle—they could dig in and hold their ground when in hand-to-hand combat.

Believers also need special "shoes"—*the readiness that comes from the gospel of peace.* The Word of God is the gospel, or Good News, that brings peace. In other words, believers are ready for battle because "the peace of God, which surpasses all understanding, will guard [their] hearts and minds through Christ Jesus" (Philippians 4:7 NKJV). They can stand firm, with peace, even in hand-to-hand combat, because they know that they are doing right and that they are on the winning side. Christians are in the battle both with the inner peace Christ has already given and the desire to produce that peace in the hearts of others. This can only happen as they share this "gospel of peace" with those who have not yet heard and accepted it.

When the enemy, the deceiver (Revelation 12:9), offers false ways to peace or tries to get us to focus on our concerns and fears, we Christian soldiers can stand up to him. Jesus promised, "Peace I leave with you, My peace I give to you; not as the world gives do I give to you. Let not your heart be troubled, neither let it be afraid" (John 14:27 NKJV).

6:16 With all of these, take the shield of faith, with which you will be able to quench all the flaming arrows of the evil one.NRSV *With all* the pieces of armor mentioned above, the soldier needed to also carry extra protection in the form of a *shield*. The image was taken from the Roman shield, a large oblong or oval piece, approximately four feet high by two feet wide, made of wood and leather, often with an iron frame. Sometimes the leather would be soaked in water to help extinguish *flaming arrows*. The ancient "flaming arrow" or "fire dart" was made of cane with a flammable head that was lighted and then shot so as to set fire to wooden shields, cloth tents, etc. For Christians, this shield is *faith*—complete reliance on God. Faith means total dependence on God and willingness to do his will. It is not something we put on for a show for others. It means believing in his promises even though we don't see those promises materializing yet. God gives faith to protect the believer (Ephesians 2:8). (See James 1:31 and Peter 1:7 for more on faith as the key to victory.)

When the enemy, the ruler of this world (John 12:31), sends his flaming arrows of temptation, doubt, wrath, lust, despair, vengeance, problems, and trials into our lives, we can hold up our shields and *quench* them. We are assured that "whatever is born of God conquers the world. And this is the victory that conquers the world, our faith" (1 John 5:4 NRSV). We must take hold of God's full resources. Faith gives us the strength to stand against Satan with firm courage, even when he uses his most fearsome weapons.

6:17 **And take the helmet of salvation.**^{NKJV} The *helmet* protected the soldier's head. Helmets were made of leather and brass, or sometimes bronze and iron—no sword could pierce a good helmet. Isaiah 59:17 describes God wearing a helmet of salvation. The dressed soldier would *take* his helmet and sword from an armor bearer. In the same way, believers are to *take* this helmet of salvation, for it is handed to them by God himself. First Thessalonians 5:8 calls believers to put on "the hope of salvation as a helmet." This "hope" is a certainty—believers have complete assurance that God will do all that he has promised. Their salvation, already accomplished, will be consummated when Christ comes to claim his own. Christians, with the assurance of salvation protecting their minds, can stand against Satan's attacks. As a blow to the head often means death, so a person without hope of salvation will be easily defeated by the enemy.

When the enemy, the devil (1 Peter 5:8), seeks to devour and destroy God's people with empty or evil thoughts, trying to get us to doubt our salvation, we can trust in the protection of the helmet. Our salvation will be accomplished, for God has promised it. "Hope does not disappoint us" (Romans 5:5 NIV) because "our salvation is nearer now than when we first believed" (Romans 13:11 NIV).

And the sword of the Spirit, which is the word of God.^{NKJV} Finally, the soldier takes *the sword of the Spirit*—the only offensive weapon mentioned. This refers to the short sword used in close combat. The sharp, short sword was one of Rome's great military innovations. The Roman army was called the "short swords" because of its use of the short swords in winning battles. The sword's double edges made it ideal for "cut and thrust" strategy. The relative pronoun translated *which* could refer to "the Spirit" or to the whole phrase, "sword of the Spirit." The Word of God is the Spirit's sword (see Isaiah 11:4-5; 2 Thessalonians 2:8; Hebrews 4:12). The Spirit makes the Word of God effective as we speak it and receive it. The Spirit gives the Word its penetrating power and sharp edge. Jesus' use of God's Word in his temptation prompts our use of it against Satan (Matthew 4:4, 7, 10). With the Holy Spirit

GOD'S ARMOR FOR US

We are engaged in a spiritual battle—all believers find themselves subject to Satan's attacks because they are no longer on Satan's side. Thus, Paul tells us to use every piece of God's armor to resist Satan's attacks and to stand true to God in the midst of those attacks.

Piece of Armor	Use	Application
Belt	Truth	Satan fights with lies, and sometimes his lies sound like truth; but only believers have God's truth, which can defeat Satan's lies.
Breastplate	Righteousness	Satan often attacks our heart—the seat of our emotions, self-worth, and trust. God's righteousness is the breastplate that protects our heart and ensures his approval. He approves of us because he loves us and sent his Son to die for us.
Shoes	Readiness to spread the Good News	Satan wants us to think that telling others the Good News is a worthless and hopeless task—the size of the task is too big and the negative responses are too much to handle. But the footgear God gives us enables us to proclaim the true peace that is available in God—news everyone needs to hear.
Shield	Faith	What we see are Satan's attacks in the form of insults, setbacks, and temptations. But the shield of faith protects us from Satan's flaming arrows. With God's perspective, we can see beyond our circumstances and know that ultimate victory is ours.
Helmet	Salvation	Satan wants to make us doubt God, Jesus, and our salvation. The helmet protects our mind from doubting God's saving work for us.
Sword	The Spirit, the Word of God	The sword is the only weapon of offense in this list of armor. There are times when we need to take the offensive against Satan. When we are tempted, we need to live in the Spirit of God's Word.

within, believers have the constant reminder of God's Word to use against Satan's temptations.

When the enemy, the tempter (Matthew 4:3-4; 1 Thessalonians 3:5), tries to tempt us to do evil, we have the power to send him away with *the word of God.* The Spirit will bring the words to mind, for Jesus promised, "The Counselor, the Holy Spirit, whom the Father will send in my name, will teach you all things and will remind you of everything I have said to you" (John 14:26 NIV).

6:18 And pray in the Spirit on all occasions with all kinds of prayers and requests. With this in mind, be alert and always keep on praying for all the saints.[NIV] This verse, although not naming another "weapon" in the believers' armor, does continue the thought of 6:17. As we take the sword of the Spirit, God's Word, we must also *pray in the Spirit on all occasions.* Praying in the Spirit means that the Spirit helps us when we pray (Romans 8:26); the Spirit prays on our behalf (Romans 8:27); the Spirit makes God accessible (Ephesians 2:18); the Spirit gives us confidence when we pray (Romans 8:15-16; Galatians 4:6). He inspires and guides us when we pray. He helps us communicate with God and also brings God's response to us.

> God has given us the total victory of the power of the cross through the weapon of prayer. Isn't it time that we covenant together to pick up that awesome weapon and use it to His glory?
>
> *Catherine Marshall*

Paul was not calling prayer a weapon; instead, he was giving the how-to's for taking up the armor described in the previous verses. We must not underestimate Satan's forces. He will strike in different ways at different people; thus, we need to pray "all kinds" of prayers, allowing for all kinds of requests. Satan will attack at various times, but he will always be attacking someone. Believers need to be praying *always.* Satan will attack when we least expect it, so we need to be *alert* to prayer needs when they arise. Satan will rarely let up if he thinks he can win the battle, so believers must *keep on* praying, no matter how long it takes. No believer is exempt from being Satan's target—Satan demands battle against his enemies (believers). Thus *all saints* need our prayer support—no matter who they are, what position they hold, or how strong they may seem to be. No believer can stand alone in this battle. For whom do you pray? How often do you pray?

How can anyone pray *on all occasions*? Make quick, brief prayers your habitual response to every situation you meet throughout the day. Order your life around God's desires and teachings so that your very life becomes a prayer. You don't have to isolate yourself from other people and from daily work in order to pray constantly. You can make prayer your life and your life a prayer while living in a world that needs God's powerful influence. This does not happen by human effort alone. Such prayers are empowered by the Holy Spirit. Only in him can we pray the effective, powerful, and timely prayers that will change the world.

AIR SUPPORT
Any military strategist will tell you that while you cannot win a war without ground troops, air superiority gives you an overwhelming advantage. Paul describes our "air support" as prayer because God's army advances on its knees. C. S. Lewis wrote: "Enemy-occupied territory—that is what the world is. Christianity is the story of how the rightful king has landed in disguise, and is calling us all to take part in a great campaign of sabotage." Doesn't it make sense to make use of our air coverage—the power of prayer?

6:19-20 **Pray also for me, so that when I speak, a message may be given to me to make known with boldness the mystery of the gospel, for which I am an ambassador in chains. Pray that I may declare it boldly, as I must speak.**^{NRSV} After asking the believers to pray for one another in the battle, he asked them to pray also for him. Paul wrote this letter as a Roman prisoner, yet his ministry could be virtually unhindered if he continued to speak the gospel message clearly. Those who understood why he was in chains and how he could trust his Lord even as he sat in prison could be drawn to the gospel. Undiscouraged and undefeated, Paul wrote powerful letters of encouragement from prison. He did not ask the Ephesians to pray that his chains would be removed but that he would continue to *speak* fearlessly for Christ even as he wore his chains. Paul asked them to pray that he could *make known with boldness the mystery of the gospel.* Paul did not depend on his own wisdom or eloquence, rather that the Spirit would inspire him with *a message* that would clearly and boldly explain the gospel.

The "boldness" Paul needed was for proclaiming the gospel message in all its truth, even before hostile audiences. The "mystery" refers to God's plan through the ages to draw both Jews and Gentiles to himself in one body, the church (see 1:9; 3:3, 6, 9; 5:32). Indeed, it was that very message that had landed Paul in prison in the first place (see Acts 22:17–23:11). Yet he considered himself *an ambassador in chains.* "Ambassador" was a political term for a government's legal representative. Paul realized that in being taken to Rome as a prisoner, he was actually acting as an ambassador for another "nation," God's kingdom.

"PRAY FOR ME"
Rather than ending his mission, Paul's imprisonment resulted in even greater possibilities for proclaiming the gospel. He asked again for prayer for boldness, adding that "I must speak." Paul had no choice but to share the gospel; he asked his fellow believers to pray for both the message and for his boldness in telling it. Do you pray for God's ambassadors? Remember to pray for missionaries and evangelists around the world as well as ministers and teachers in your church. Pray that they will be fearless in the presentation of God's Good News.

PAUL'S FINAL GREETINGS / 6:21-24

Paul closed this letter to the Ephesians and the surrounding churches by sending greetings from Rome and the Christians there. The Roman Christians and the Ephesian Christians were brothers and sisters because of their unity in Christ. Believers today are also linked to others across cultural, economic, and social barriers. All believers are one family in Christ Jesus.

6:21-22 So that you also may know how I am and what I am doing, Tychicus will tell you everything. He is a dear brother and a faithful minister in the Lord.NRSV Tychicus is also mentioned in Acts 20:4; Colossians 4:7; 2 Timothy 4:12; and Titus 3:12. He carried this letter to the Ephesians, as well as the one to the Colossians (and probably the one to Philemon as well). Tychicus acted as Paul's *dear brother and a faithful minister* bringing news about Paul to the Ephesian church, which would be very interested in hearing how Paul was doing. Paul had lived in Ephesus for three years and had become very close to the believers there (see Acts 20:17-38). Paul did not write of all those details in his letter because this letter was meant to go to several churches in the area (see the Introduction). Instead, he would allow Tychicus to *tell* the Ephesian believers *everything.*

I am sending him to you for just this purpose. He will let you know how we are, and he will encourage you.NLT Paul wanted Tychicus to encourage the believers, for it seems that they were discouraged by Paul's imprisonment (3:13). Paul wanted them to know that his imprisonment was resulting in great things for the worldwide church. News from a man who had just been at Paul's side and loved Paul the way they did would certainly *encourage* the believers.

6:23 Peace be to the whole community, and love with faith, from God the Father and the Lord Jesus Christ.NRSV Paul closed his letter with a benediction for *the whole community* of believers, using words that he had discussed in this letter. He prayed that they would have *peace* (1:2; 2:14-15, 17; 4:3; 6:15). He knew they had *faith,* but he prayed that *love* would accompany it (1:4, 15; 2:4; 3:17-19; 4:2, 15-16; 5:2, 25, 28, 33). The source of peace, love, and faith is *God the Father and the Lord Jesus Christ.*

6:24 May God's grace be upon all who love our Lord Jesus Christ with an undying love.[NLT] As he began his letter (1:2), so he ended it. Paul's final prayer was for *God's grace* upon his readers, a topic he had also written about in this letter (see also 1:6; 2:5, 7-8; 3:2, 7-8; 4:7). God's grace can only be upon those *who love our Lord Jesus Christ with an undying love.* Such love for our Lord is a taste of the eternal life of love that is our guaranteed inheritance.

BIBLIOGRAPHY

Barth, Marcus. *Ephesians: Introduction, Translation, and Commentary on Chapters 1–3, The Anchor Bible.* Garden City, N.Y.: Doubleday & Company, Inc., 1974.

————. *Ephesians: Introduction, Translation, and Commentary on Chapters 4–6, The Anchor Bible.* Garden City, N.Y.: Doubleday & Company, Inc., 1974.

Bauer, Walter, William F. Arndt, Wilbur F. Gingrich, and Frederick Danker. *A Greek-English Lexicon of the New Testament and Other Early Christian Literature.* Chicago: University of Chicago Press, 1979.

Beers, V. Gilbert. *The Victor Handbook of Bible Knowledge.* Wheaton, Ill.: Victor Books, 1981.

Bruce, F. F. *The Epistles to the Colossians, to Philemon, and to the Ephesians,* New International Commentary on the New Testament. Grand Rapids: Eerdmans, 1984.

Douglas, J. D., and Philip W. Comfort, eds. *New Commentary on the Whole Bible:* New Testament Volume. Wheaton, Ill.: Tyndale House, 1990.

Fee, Gordon D. *God's Empowering Presence: The Holy Spirit in the Letters of Paul.* Peabody, Mass.: Hendrickson Publishers, 1994.

Foulkes, Francis. *The Letter of Paul to the Ephesians,* Tyndale New Testament Commentaries. Grand Rapids: Eerdmans, 1988.

Hunter, Archibald M. *Galatians, Ephesians, Philippians, Colossians,* The Layman's Bible Commentary, vol. 22. Atlanta: John Knox Press, 1982.

Patzia, Arthur G. *Ephesians, Colossians, Philemon,* New International Biblical Commentary. Peabody, Mass.: Hendrickson Publishers, 1990.

Walvoord, John F., and Roy B. Zuck. *Bible Knowledge Commentary:* New Testament Edition. Wheaton, Ill.: Victor Books, 1983.

Wood, A. Skevington. "Ephesians," *The Expositor's Bible Commentary,* vol. 11. Frank E. Gaebelein, ed. Grand Rapids: Zondervan, 1978.

INDEX